Tailoring Suits the Professional Way

Tailoring Suits

The Professional Way

Revised

By CLARENCE POULIN

B

CHAS. A. BENNETT CO., INC.

Peoria, Illinois 61614

To a master craftsman,
my teacher for seven years,
Mr. Dosithé Dragon

Contents

Introduction

THIS book aims to present in understandable, simple language the series of operations a tailor follows in making up coats, trousers, vests, and skirts. It is addressed both to apprentices in the trade and to lay students, and the instructions apply to the production of both men's and women's suits.

While modern mass-production methods of turning out garments have greatly depleted the ranks of custom tailors and coat makers, popular interest in their old and honored craft is still much in evidence. Aside from the considerable number of tailors whose services remain in demand, many women outside the trade are finding a creative outlet — and a truly remunerative one — in making suits and coats for their own use.

At the start, may I express my concern that so few of those at the helm of education in this country have interested themselves in promoting the study of tailoring in the schools. In view of the facts that a serious shortage of tailors now exists in the United States, that the study of tailoring can serve a real need in the field of occupational therapy and rehabilitation, and that many boys and girls can be prepared to earn an interesting, independent livelihood at the craft, it would seem desirable to promote the study of garment making as we do that of other manual subjects.

The reason that tailoring has been neglected is obvious; it is not an easy trade to learn. In the past, apprentices have had to serve a minimum of five years under a master tailor before being accounted competent to start on their own. The subject

11

matter involves innumerable details of technique which can be grasped only in the course of close instructor-student rapport. Still, the central problem in teaching tailoring, as that in the teaching of any other craft, can be largely solved by stripping the subject to its bare essentials.

From the earliest days of my apprenticeship, I searched for trade books that would simplify for me matters that seemed more complex than necessary. I wanted to learn faster ways of working, more analyzable methods of drafting; obtain a clearer understanding of the mechanics of the coat. In short, I wanted to perfect myself through understanding the basic principles. I read a great many books, but I found none that seemed satisfactorily written from the viewpoint of the apprentice.

This manual, it is my hope, will be to other beginners the book of fundamentals that I searched for in those days. It ought to be so for three reasons: (1) It presents a common basis on which to design men's and women's coats, and the beginner is purposely confined to a single formula on whose lines he can produce a coat for any near-normal figure. (2) It explains in detail the procedure in fitting, a most important subject usually far too briefly handled by authors. (3) It shows all basic operations in clear, step-by-step diagrams accompanied by concise instructions. Lengthy word descriptions, which seldom succeed at communicating the details of garment construction, are purposely omitted.

Although coat making is discussed first of all in these pages, and should be studied first of all in order to obtain a mental grasp of the subject, I should certainly not plunge a beginner immediately into coat making. All the problems involved in coats would only discourage him. I should first teach him the use of the tools, the various stitches, and then have him make for himself a pair of trousers (in the case of a woman student, a skirt, or a pair of slacks). Creativeness and the effort to succeed are always strongly stimulated when students make their first garments for themselves.

After my student had succeeded with a simple garment, I

should take advantage of his aroused self-confidence to start him making a coat — again, one for his own use.

It is by using such psychology, proving to the learner that he can make garments, and by leading him step by step from simple to harder tasks, that tailoring is most effectively taught.

As regards coats, I would warn the novice not to expect to make one in half a day. It can't be done. It takes an experienced craftsman 2½ long work days (or 24 hours of labor) to make up a good coat. Plan on giving your first coat as much time as you need to make every part of it the very best possible. Do things step by step, don't look far ahead; and, most important, be patient. The first job is bound to be long and hard, but each succeeding one will be easier and better.

Make up your first coat on the simplest pattern obtainable, and from a piece of plain goods, such as a substantial, 14-ounce cheviot. If you are an impatient sort of individual, make as few pockets as possible. Women students can make pocketless coats of normal appearance by making up flaps and sewing them in the proper position so that they suggest real pockets.

Under the method of study outlined here, drafting is the first thing to learn. Don't let the formulas frighten you; they look far more formidable than they really are. As soon as you have made a few drafts, you will see that they are quite simple.

I have limited the scope of these chapters to the normal or near-normal figure; therefore drafting systems for corpulent figures and alterations for major abnormalities are not given. Some limitation is necessary in a work for beginners.

The chapters that follow teach only one way of doing each of the various operations, and present them in a sequence suited to the needs of beginners. There are other methods of working which arrive at the same ends.

All line illustrations in this book are reproductions of pencil drawings originated by the author in the course of actual shop practice. Pen-and-ink renderings of all the drawings are the work of Mrs. Marjorie Rowell Sturm of Concord, who greatly improved them artistically.

PREFACE TO THE THIRD EDITION

It is now twenty years since this book first appeared—certainly a sufficiently long time for either its usefulness or its defects to have become apparent. As its author, I have naturally been gratified that it has been found useful in many trade schools where its lessons have been subjected to rigid testing. But it is also for this reason that requests for needed additions and changes cannot be ignored.

The entire chapter on trousers has been rewritten to feature construction with the zipper closure rather than buttons. Women students have asked for a formula for a fitted suit jacket; I have tried to present as fine a draft as I could devise. A new and better draft for the man's jacket and a new skirt formula also appear. In addition, I felt that I would not complete the revision adequately unless I gave some instruction on the grading of patterns. Several other changes and additions, which students of the original text will notice readily, will, I believe, prove helpful.

My sincere thanks go to Mr. Alec Nicholas for his pains and artistry in rendering some forty new drawings in pen and ink.

Figs. 22 (a, b, and c), 207 and 208 and 209 to 216 are reproduced from my publication "Supplementary Lessons in Women's and Men's Suit Tailoring," copyright 1962.

Chapter I

What Is Good Tailoring

Just as a carpenter must bear in his mind an idealized image of the house which he is about to build, must acquaint himself with the details of a well-built house, so must the tailor be able to visualize the features of a well-constructed garment. It seems like simple knowledge to acquire, yet many persons who earn their livings by sewing do not really know what a good garment should look like. They never improve for lack of an ideal to aspire toward.

If you want to tailor, you want to tailor well. Poor work, mediocre work, brings no satisfaction. You are going to use good taste, and take pains to do everything as well as it can be done.

As a first exercise, I recommend that you examine a well-tailored coat.

Note, first, that *the edges are thin* even where you would expect the seams to pile up thickly at their junctions. Thinness at the junction of seams is what all good tailors strive at. There are no bumps or slovenly, thick areas along the edges of a good coat.

Note also that *the edges all curl slightly inward,* never outward. This applies to the fronts, the sleeve vents, the pocket flaps, the revers, and the corners of the collar. Everything curls slightly inward; nothing sticks out.

A good coat has straight seams and straight edges all over.

There are no crooks or puckers. The front edge is smooth, and not stretched at any point. All seams are well pressed open from the inside.

Linings are always loosely put in so that they do not interfere with the drape of the coat when worn.

Buttons are sewn with a "neck," and not too tightly, so as to avoid puckering about their bases. The buttonholes are handmade, and are not hard.

The hand-sewing around the collar and elsewhere is even and inconspicuous.

The sleeves hang clean with no diagonal flutings. The collar sits close around the neck but is neither tight nor loose. The fronts and the revers have a narrow stitching along their edges.

A good garment is not necessarily a custom or tailor-made garment, or even one almost completely hand-sewn. Many firms are now manufacturing ready-made garments which, with all their machined seams, are beautifully proportioned and durably made in every detail.

As an aspiring tailor, you should pay close attention to the cut, fit, and workmanship in all the garments that you have a chance to examine. Only by recognizing the features of a superior coat can you hope to create with your hands the perfect article which you see in your mind.

A question frequently asked is, just what makes a custom tailored suit superior to one ready-made? The answer is, mainly its better fit. A tailored suit may not be made of better woolens than a high grade commercial one, but if it was constructed by a good craftsman it should fit better than the ready-made one. It is very true, of course, that the person who is symmetrically built and of normal posture may obtain a perfect fit in the commercial garment. But very many people, perhaps most of them, are not symmetrical. Even the well proportioned often have slight defects, such as a low shoulder, large blades, or a forward neck, that make it hard for them to obtain a good fit. It is such people who can appreciate the superiority of fine custom tailored garments.

Chapter II

Tools and Their Uses

IN TAILORING, as in other crafts, success largely depends on using the proper tools. Indeed, using the right tools is what makes the craft enjoyable as well as remunerative. Using the wrong ones is what makes it disagreeable. So, at the start, know what you will need in your tailoring room. These articles you may obtain from a tailor's supply house, or from any merchant tailor.

You will need:

NEEDLES, in at least two sizes: No. 5 Betweens, the larger size, are 1½ in. long and are used mainly for basting, sewing buttons, and other work requiring coarse thread. No. 6 Betweens, the smaller size, are 1⅜ in. long and are used in all hand sewing. Some tailors prefer a No. 3 or 4 for basting, but most find the No. 5 large enough. Use only these short needles, even though they seem hard to handle at first. The long, thin needles usually sold in stores are unsatisfactory.

THREADS, in both mercerized cotton for machine sewing, and in silk for hand sewing. For hand sewing, silk is preferable to cotton because it is smoother and won't gnarl so readily, and because it has resilience or "give" and will stretch with the garment. "Hand-sewing silk" is sold as such (distinguished from machine silk, which is finer) and spools of it in size O, in black, white, and several colors, should be on hand at all times. Machine silk or mercerized cotton (you may use either on the machine, though the silk is, of course, preferable) should be had in five different shades of gray, three of brown, and three of tan, as these are the most used colors. On extremely dark blue or brown cloth, black thread may be used. Odd colors in blue, green, red, or purple may be bought in small dime spools as they are needed. All mercerized cotton is bought in size O.

BASTING THREAD. This is smooth, strong, white cotton thread in size 40.

BUTTON THREAD. Obtainable in cotton or linen, of which the last is preferable, and should be had in black, medium and light gray, brown, and tan.

BUTTONHOLE TWIST. Is heavy silk wound eight strands together on the spool, especially designed for the working of buttonholes and the making of "tacks" at the ends of pockets, etc. It should also be had in a variety of colors, in size 10 for general work in suits. As it is expensive, it may be purchased by the yard as well as by spool from tailors' supply houses.

A THIMBLE. Tailor's thimbles are sold in various sizes, and designed open at the end, i.e., without a top.

SHEARS. For general work, a 9 or 10 in. shear is satisfactory. It is necessary that the handle be bent for cutting on the table, and absolutely essential that the points cut sharp and clean.

BEESWAX. Most beginners don't realize the time saved through the habitual use of this wax on their thread, and dislike to sew by hand because they are always struggling with gnarls and knots. Running the thread against the wax and smoothing it with the fingers is the solution to this problem.

A SPONGE. Used with only a moderate amount of water in it to wet the seams before ironing them open with the flatiron in direct contact with the cloth.

A BODKIN. A small bone pencil with a smooth point, used to draw out bastings. The end of an old crotchet needle makes a good one.

A SMALL POCKETKNIFE. One with a small blade kept not too sharp is best to rip seams with. A razor blade is too sharp and unwieldy for this purpose.

TAILOR'S CHALK. Used to mark on cloth, and differs from ordinary chalk in the ease with which it can be brushed off.

A PAPER OF PINS.

A FOOT RULER, YARDSTICK, and TAPE-MEASURE.

A TAILOR'S SQUARE, if you plan to draft your patterns.

A FULL-LENGTH MIRROR, preferably in three panels, so that one can see one's back in it.

A FORM or dummy on which to place coats when setting collars and sleeves.

A SLEEVEBOARD (sometimes called duplex board). This article you can manufacture yourself or buy ready-made. A useful sleeveboard measures about 35 in. in length, is 10 in. wide at the large end, 4¾ in. wide at the small end, and 7½ in. high. Its upper board is padded with two layers of cotton felt, covered with a piece of woolen suiting cloth tacked from underneath the edges all around. It must be covered smoothly, drawing the cloth tightly while tacking it.

A BEATER. This is a board of hardwood, smooth and well rounded at the edges, about a foot long, 4½ in. wide at the large end, 3½ in. wide at the small end, and 1 in. thick. This is such a simple tool that the beginner never appreciates its utility until it is proven by demonstration. The beater is used whenever an especially sharp crease or flat press is wanted, to aid in subduing material which refuses to respond in the usual way. It is applied emphatically immediately after the iron is lifted, and kept onto the part about half a minute, to keep the steam working longer in the cloth.

A PRESS CLOTH. A piece of ordinary, medium-weight bed sheeting, out of which the starch has been washed, will do. It should be about 1 yd. square. Be certain that it contains no starch, or the hot iron will get stuck to it and will become encrusted with a film of burnt starch which is difficult to remove.

A FLATIRON. Any good household iron can do, but it is best to have a tailor's iron with three heats — low, medium, and hot; and, in weight, anything from 8 to 15 pounds — that is, as heavy as the strength of the user will permit.

A Sewing Machine. A standard tailor's machine is preferable, though for suitmaking almost any strong household machine may serve. The machine should be equipped with a small clamp through which a metal gage may be inserted to govern the width of edge seams. The tailor's machine is more difficult to thread than the ordinary machine, but one quickly gets used to its features.

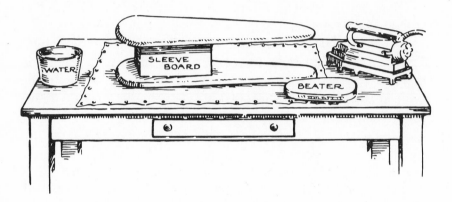

FIG. 1. The tailoring bench and arrangement.

A Bench. Have your bench at least 3 ft. wide by 6 ft. long and perfectly straight and smooth, as you will not only cut on it but press as well. To insure evenness of the boards, reinforce them from underneath with cross-boards fastened with plenty of screws. In the center of the bench, spread a layer of cotton felt 4 ft. long by 3 ft. wide, and cover it with a piece of pocket drilling or other smooth, strong cloth, which is to be tacked firmly all around. On this surface, you will be able to press all flat work, thus eliminating the need of a cheeseblock.

For illumination, a 100-watt light in metal reflector, suspended rather low over the bench, is well suited. It is also advisable that the electric socket for the flatiron be equipped with a red pilot bulb, so that the tailor will be visually reminded when the electricity is on, and be spared the consequence of quitting the room with the iron heating.

USING THE SEWING MACHINE

Taking long seams

Practice taking long seams on two layers of cloth of similar lengths, with the view of finishing the seams with the ends coinciding. This is an important technique to master because of the tendency of all sewing machines to "full in" the lower layer of cloth, thus causing the upper layer to extend beyond at the end of the seam. This fulling in of the lower layer is caused by its contact with the dented plate of the machine, which forces the cloth to travel forward while the upper layer of cloth is held back by the stationary foot bearing down on it. This action of the machine is overcome by pulling forward the lower layer with the right hand while pushing back the upper layer with the left. With practice, one soon learns how to do this.

Sewing backward

Practice sewing backward as well as frontward, as it is necessary to begin and end most seams with a few back-and-forth stitches to fasten the ends. One can sew backward on almost any machine by lifting the foot lever a little with the right hand while pushing the cloth backward with the left hand; then letting the lever fall in its natural position when it is desired to have the cloth go forward. It will be found that the lever must be lifted just to the correct extent, and that the needle must be inserted properly, if back-stitching is to be possible. Any slight diagonal position of the needle hole will cause the thread to break.

Starting a seam

In starting a seam, always hold down the ends of both upper and lower threads with the index finger of the right hand, as leaving the ends loose will result in their being lost or becoming gnarled. Start and end all seams with a few back-and-forth stitches, else they will soon unfasten at the ends. In

21

sewing a piece of lining to one of cloth (as in making pocket flaps or topcoat cuffs), the lining must be on top of the cloth, and never under it.

Adjusting thread tension

Also learn to adjust the tensions of the threads on the machine, as loose "running" seams result from dissimilar tensions between the upper thread and that of the shuttle. These tensions are controlled: for the upper thread, by adjustment of the tension screw on the head; for the lower thread, by adjustment of the screw which tightens the spring of the shuttle.

Automatic bobbin winder

Tailors' machines are fitted with a bobbin-winder to the right of the head which winds the bobbin while the operator is sewing and which automatically releases it when it is filled. When it is necessary to fill a bobbin while not sewing, be sure to lift the foot lever to save it from unnecessary grinding on the plate.

Chapter III

Hand-Sewing Technique

IF YOU turn a well tailored coat inside out and examine the sewing around the armhole, you will see that it was done by hand with very fine, even stitches. If, then, you will examine the seam along the base of the collar, you will find an even less visible and a much neater hand-sewn seam. The stitch used in these parts is the common hand-felling or "hemming" stitch. In appearance it is much like the overcasting stitch shown in Fig. 5, except that the seam is worked in the opposite direction. To master this basic stitch, practice hand-felling any turned-in edge such as a skirt hem or a trouser bottom.

Tailor's knot

First of all, learn to tie a tailor's knot — sometimes called a weaver's knot — at the end of your length of thread. This is done with the thumb and index finger of the right hand. Grasp the thread end between these two fingers, loop around index, rolling thread end through the loop with a forward push of the thumb. A knot of this kind is tied in a split second without even looking, and it is an extremely simple trick to learn.

Thread lengths

Cut your thread lengths not much longer than 36 in. These very long lengths that beginners always like to take only get tangled and waste time.

Waxing

Wax the thread by drawing it across a piece of beeswax two or three times, afterward smoothing it by passing it through the fingers. This is your guarantee against gnarls and knots.

The needle and thimble

Use a No. 6 needle, which is neither too large nor too small. And wear a thimble. Beginners all have a prejudice against thimbles, and many cannot be induced to wear one until they have pricked the middle finger of the right hand into a bloody mess. Wear the thimble even if it is harder to sew with it than without it. It goes on the third finger of the right hand, and the needle is pushed against its side very close to the lower edge.

Sewing method

Sew *toward* yourself — not away from yourself. This means that each stitch is taken in front (toward yourself) of the previous stitch. At first, you will have difficulty making the stitches even and fine. Don't worry too much about that; skill will come in time. A beginner's seam, even if uneven, can be as strong and durable as that of the best tailor in the world. In making, say, a skirt hem, a good craftsman inserts the needle under the raw edge of the cloth, takes up only one thread of the lower layer, and then only about ⅛ in. of the upper layer. Do not pull the thread tightly, else the stitches will show from the outside of the hem you are making. Most novices, especially men students, have an idea that the tighter their stitching the stronger it must be. The truth is that good garments are "hung" together with resilient, fairly loose stitches, not "nailed" so tightly that the seams refuse to give with the rest of the cloth.

Attempting to hold your work properly in the hand is another thing that will embarrass you at first; but this, as with other things, will come to you with practice.

In sewing, the best posture to adopt is the traditional cross-legged one, used from time immemorial in the trade. The tailor sits on his bench, his work supported on his knees, which are at just about the most comfortable distance from his eyes and his hands. Contrary to general opinion, this is a much more comfortable posture than the bent and cramped one that must be assumed in sitting on a chair.

Sew always with silk thread, size A, if available. Silk is strong, elastic, and does not gnarl easily. If silk is not available use a strong mercerized cotton well smoothed with wax.

Finishing seams

Tailors end a hand seam not by tying a knot but by taking five or six stitches on top of one another, afterward breaking the thread.

Other stitches that every tailoring student must learn are the following:

THE STITCHES

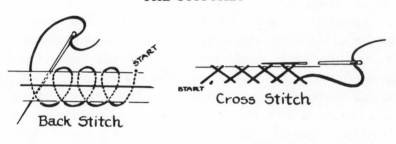

Back Stitch

Cross Stitch

FIG. 2.   FIG. 3.

The back stitch

Before the invention of the sewing machine, all seams were sewn by hand using the back stitch. Now it is used only where an especially strong seam is desired, such as along the center-back seam of trousers, and sometimes in sewing the sleeves into the armhole. The stitches are taken from left to right, the needle pointing always toward the left, as shown in Fig. 2.

The cross stitch

This stitch is occasionally used instead of the felling stitch, as in hemming skirts. The tailor sews from left to right, the needle pointing toward the left. Fig. 3.

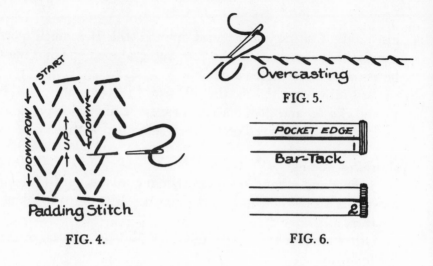

Overcasting

FIG. 5.

Padding Stitch

FIG. 4.

POCKET EDGE

Bar-Tack

FIG. 6.

The padding stitch

This is a very useful stitch, utilized in fastening the canvas to the facing of the revers, the collar canvas onto the under-collar, and the haircloth to the canvas interlining. On the inside of the garment, padding shows as vertical rows of diagonal stitches; from the outside, as a series of very faint pricks. The sewing is done in up-and-down rows, the needle being inserted horizontally toward the left. Stitches are rather loose and about ¾ in. long. Fig. 4.

The overcasting stitch

An ordinary felling stitch which is run along the raw edges of a newly cut garment to prevent ravelling of the raw edges. Fig. 5.

The bar-tack

Is used to reinforce the ends of the mouths of pockets, and is made with buttonhole silk twist. A bar-tack is made of three bar stitches, Fig. 6 (1), around which rotary prick stitches are worked the entire length (2).

The invisible tack

These tacks are made entirely from the reverse of the garment using a series of close back stitches, which do not quite penetrate to the outside of the pocket. They are used to reinforce the corners of the welt of the outside breast pocket.

The prick or through stitch

Where the back stitch cannot be used because of the thickness of the material, one must prick the needle back and forth through the cloth, downward and upward in alternation. One uses this stitch in sewing on buttons and in making the triangular tack at the base of the trouser fly. From the outside of the garment, prick stitches appear as a series of dots.

Buttonhole making

At first, buttonholes are difficult to make, but with practice one readily gains proficiency at them.

Use No. 10 twist in silk a trifle darker than the cloth on which they are to be worked. For an average ¾ in. hole, cut strands about 30 in. in length, wax them thoroughly, and then run the hot iron over them to make them stiff and gnarlproof.

Your buttonholes must be worked on a "cord," which is a double and twisted length of button thread, laid and held tautly along the edge of the hole as you work. The cord gives the hole body, keeps its edge short and firm, and raises the purls on an even line. *No hole can be built properly without using such a foundation cord.*

Buttonholes may be cut with a special punch which cuts both the straight portion and the eye at once; or they may be cut with small, sharp-pointed scissors. In the latter case, the eye is cut in the shape of a small triangle. Fig. 7, page 28.

All holes are cut ⅛ in. wider than the button which is to go through them.

Once cut, the holes are overcast all around with fine thread to fasten their edges together. Fig. 8, page 28.

The cord (which is threaded on a No. 5 needle) is entered between the layers of cloth as at A, Fig. 9, emerging at B, in line with the end of the buttonhole. The knot of the cord is at A, while its other end, C, is attached to some stationary object,

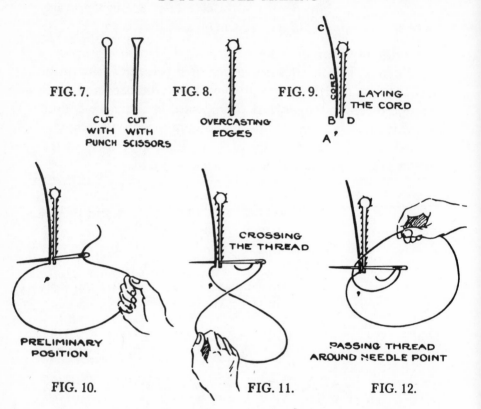

FIG. 7.

CUT WITH PUNCH CUT WITH SCISSORS

FIG. 8.

OVERCASTING EDGES

FIG. 9.

LAYING THE CORD

PRELIMINARY POSITION

FIG. 10.

CROSSING THE THREAD

FIG. 11.

PASSING THREAD AROUND NEEDLE POINT

FIG. 12.

so that it may be held taut while working. The cord is, of course, longer than shown in the diagram, a 30 in. length being suitable. As one works, it is made to follow the edge of the hole, and when the hole has been stitched to the end, at D, the cord is passed again between the layers of cloth, and cut about ¾ in. beyond point D. Then the knot, A, is cut also. Thus, the ends of the cord are free and not tied between the layers of cloth.

The stitching of the buttonhole commences at the left side of the hole. Figs. 10, 11, and 12 show the three successive movements required to make a stitch. Following the last movement, all that is necessary to make the purl is to grasp the needle by the point and pull it directly upward. To look well, the stitches should be taken at about the same depth and the same distance apart. Facility is acquired with practice.

When the hole is stitched all around, the end is worked in the manner of a small bar-tack, the same as is used on pocket ends. Then the hole is basted closed with three or four stitches so that it will not gape open after pressing. It is a good idea to rotate the point of the bodkin in the eye of the hole to round it out neatly.

Basting

If you wish to produce nice garments, do not be stingy with your bastings. Basting is tedious, but liberal basting is indispensable to a high standard of work. A bench-tailored coat at the near-completion stage, is a truly awesome mass of bastings, but each of them has a vitally important function.

Get in the habit of basting on the bench, whenever that is possible on the particular part you are doing. Basting in the hand results in crooked, uneven work which must often be ripped apart and done over. On the bench, you can fasten one layer of cloth onto another in the exact position you want it to lie when finally sewn.

Basting stitches are taken rather loosely, 1½ to 2 in. apart. It is their location which is important, not their appearance as stitches.

Preparing a cord

For sewing buttons and to serve as foundation in buttonholes, always use a doubled, twisted length of button thread. Thread the needle with a two-yard length of it, draw the ends together and knot them thus. Stick the needle in the sleeve-board or other stationary object, and holding the doubled thread taut by the knotted end, start twisting it toward your left, or counter-clockwise. After you have it well twisted the entire length, rub it thoroughly with beeswax, afterward smoothing it with a bit of cloth or under the hot iron.

Chapter IV
Pressing

PRESSING is hard work, especially with thin or obstinate cloths, and it requires a good deal of practice to become a good pressman. But the rewards are well worth the pains, for pressing is to the coat what a bright, fresh coat of paint is to a newly built house. It sets off all the good points of the finished garment while concealing minor defects.

The first consideration in pressing is to have the flatiron at the right heat. When started, the iron should be switched on *high*, but when it gets quite hot it is turned to *medium* or to *low*, for the remainder of the pressing period. The iron is at the right heat when water splashed on it sizzles back sharply. The tailor also knows when it gets too hot by the speed with which it dries out the moisture in the cloth. In case it does so very fast, it will stick to the cloth and may scorch the garment.

When the iron is not hot enough, it does not move easily along the surface of the press cloth but sticks to it and steams rather than presses the coat. Most beginners have trouble moving the iron without its dragging the press cloth because they lift the iron before the cloth is sufficiently dry. A little patience and perseverance will teach them correct methods in this matter.

Frequently lift the press cloth from the garment to see what is happening to it. Too brief a contact with the iron will leave the cloth wet and unpressed in appearance; too long contact

30

will make it shiny. Learn to set the iron in one place just long enough to flatten the material without shining it. Shine, or gloss, however, is nothing to worry about as far as its removal is concerned, for it readily disappears when the area involved is re-steamed. The one thing to fear and avoid is scorching, and, to prevent it, keep your iron never too long in one place.

In pressing, have only as much water in the press cloth as will not wring out with strenuous twisting. More water than is necessary makes the work harder and longer, due to the longer evaporation needed.

It will soon be noted that cloths vary greatly in pressing quality; soft, full-bodied cloths of good quality responding readily to the iron, while thin, hard, or wiry ones (like tropicals, and some gabardines and serges) will be obstinate and require a dry press. Indeed, some cloths cannot be pressed flat without drying them close to the shiny stage; and, of course, you must be extremely careful not to scorch them at that stage. The iron must be kept moving and not too hot. It will be found that applying the beater to such obstinate cloths will cause them to yield readily.

Old creases will press out if enough steam is applied with a not-too-hot iron.

Additional instructions on pressing will follow in the section on coat making, and elsewhere.

Note on scorches

Scorches — that terror of tailors — if they involve only the surface of the cloth, are removable with salts of lemon, obtainable at all drugstores. This inexpensive white powder has performed so many miracles for me that I cannot recommend it too highly. Simply mix the powder with water, into a paste, rubbing onto and into the scorched area. Rub it thoroughly and briskly for a few minutes; then expose to the sun for an hour or so. Finally, wash off the area in plenty of clear water and allow to dry. If the scorch still shows, repeat the process.

Chapter V

Cloths and Trimmings

CHOICE AND PREPARATION OF MATERIALS

Cloths are sold folded lengthwise, measuring thus 27 to 30 in.; or spread out, 54 to 60 in. The cloth is folded wrong side out, so that the tailor may cut it on the double, as he must do to obtain two identical foreparts, backparts, sleeves, etc. Thus, the cut-out pieces lie right side to right side. All cloths as purchased should measure 37 in. to the yard length, the extra inch being allowed for shrinkage.

Cloths marked shrunk are often only partly so, and in all cases the tailor takes no chances of cutting them before shrinking them himself. He does this by rolling up the cloth in a length of dampened sheeting, and allowing it to set thus for two hours. For shrinking, ordinary cheap cotton bed sheets torn in half give lengths of the proper width. Wet the sheeting and wring it out thoroughly. Then lay one end of the cloth on the bench, allowing the rest to fall frontward at your feet. Lay the sheeting on it in the same way. Place a board 6 in. wide by 32 in. long on the end of the sheeting and start rolling (toward yourself) the cloth and the sheeting together around the board. When all the cloth is thus rolled, place the sleeve board on it to assure contact with the damp sheeting, and allow it to set that way. No wrinkles should be permitted in the cloth or the sheeting as one winds them around the board; and, when removed, the cloth should be neatly spread out on the bench and allowed to dry.

Cloths vary in weight, being designated anything from 8 oz. to 24 oz. and over. The most convenient weight for men's suiting for year-round wear is 14 oz., and the beginner in tailoring does well to choose cloth of this weight. For women's suiting, 13 or 12 oz. goods is heavy enough.

Cloths also vary greatly in wool quality, and consequently in tailoring quality. "All wool" does not necessarily mean good material, or material that will tailor well; for goods thus marked are often largely made of re-used wool or shoddy. Students should practice feeling a wide variety of cloths with the fingers, to learn to recognize the characteristic resilience or "aliveness" of high-grade woolens.

Cloths vary, too, in finish and weave, some being loosely woven, some tightly, some in the manner of a basket, others in that of a twill pattern; some being finely finished without nap, others left unfinished. The beginner is advised to favor a twill weave with an unfinished or nappy surface, as defects in workmanship do not readily show up in such material.

TWEEDS, which are unfinished, twilled fabrics, are easiest to work of all cloths. However, garments made out of them should be cut rather on the small size, as the fabric is stretchable. Beginners' mistakes, such as crooked seams, and clumsy buttonholes and tacks, do not show up in this material, and it shapes up readily under the flatiron.

SERGE, which is a firm, twilled fabric, is a desirable cloth for the novice who is bent on doing good work and wants it to show up. Serge does not stretch easily, and has plenty of body; and a garment properly made from it is always neat and durable.

CHEVIOT, a rough twill, but finer than tweed, tailors exquisitely, and requires a minimum of fussing.

Gabardine is not to be recommended, as even experienced craftsmen often have trouble with it. It can be shrunken in hardly at all and is difficult to press. Besides, the smallest crook in the seams or unevenness in cutting shows up glaringly. It is a beautiful cloth, finely finished and very tempting to beginners, but it is as dangerous as it is attractive.

Flannel is also not to be recommended, as it has little body, and its limpness makes fitting quite difficult.

In purchasing cloth, do not try to get along with barely enough. It is far cheaper in the long run to have cloth left over than to waste time trying to get all the parts out of a too-short length. An average woman's suit (coat and skirt) takes about 3 yds. (1¾ yds. for the coat, 1¼ yds. for the skirt); a large woman's about 3½ yds. For the average man's suit, 3½ yds. of cloth usually suffices: 2 yds. for the coat, 1⅓ yds. for the trousers, and the fraction left over for the vest. These quantities hold only when the cloth is of generous width — about 58 in.

A coat with a full lining requires 1¾ yds. of lining, the same material being used for the sleeves as for the body. The commonly used lining material nowadays is rayon, 40 in. wide and of a hue which matches the garment closely. Although coats are not fully lined in the ready-made trade, but only half or quarter lined, the fully lined coat always has the advantage of being less likely to wrinkle in the back and less prone to gather over the buttocks. Also the edges of the seams (since these are not piped) do not show through the coat. Nor is the coat warmer when completely lined with rayon (which is a very cool material) than is the coat with a part lining.

Rayon linings need not be shrunk, and are used as bought.

Other trimmings required for the suit coat are: ¾ yd. of silesia or pocketing, preferably of a hue somewhat near that of the garment (to safeguard against possible unfastness of dye); ½ yd. of wigan; 2 yds. of staytape; three No. 30 buttons for the fronts, and six No. 24 ones for the sleeves; also, some white cotton felt and wadding. The canvas cannot very well be bought in fractional-yard quantity, so 1 yd. can be ordered. Also, ½ yd. haircloth. While it is good practice for students to cut and make up their own canvases, these may also be bought ready-made from any tailors' supply house, in any size, at about

$1.50 per pair. While such canvases usually need altering, they are convenient to use, since they eliminate buying trimmings in larger-than-necessary quantity. Ready-made canvases come with the haircloth, felt, and the collar canvas attached. They should always be preshrunk by dipping in water and allowing to dry.

For a trouser, the trimmings required are: a 30-in. length of trouser pocketing, which is a material about 30 in. wide unfolded; a $\frac{1}{5}$ yd. length of waistband canvas, to be divided into two strips $3\frac{1}{2}$ in. wide; a similar length of waistband lining; one No. 24 button that matches the garment, six or seven fly buttons, and six suspender buttons.

For a vest, the trimmings needed are: wigan, a length the size of the forepart, silesia for the four pockets, staytape for the front edges, and six No. 24 buttons.

The trimmings for a skirt are: a strip of wigan about 2 in. wide to sew inside the belt, a 7-in. zipper, one No. 24 button, and some thin bias binding to sew along the raw edge of the hem.

Chapter VI

Pattern Drafting

ROLE AND LIMITATIONS OF PATTERNS

Beginners in tailoring almost always give credence to the theory that if you draft an accurate pattern, you will necessarily produce a perfectly fitting coat. Their hope and aim is to eliminate all fitting work and altering problems through correct designing. The truth is, however, that no matter what pains are taken to obtain perfectly accurate measurements and to draft a flawless pattern from them, some changes will have to be made in the coat cut on it. The reasons for this are two:

(1) It is virtually impossible to take precise measurements on the human body, which is ever in motion, however slight.

(2) It is impossible to prevent cloth from stretching a bit this way or that in making up a coat, or to act in other ways that defy analysis. Cloths behave differently, and tailors manipulate their work differently. I am reminded of a case where three coats, cut from the same pattern and assigned to three tailors, came out looking all different, and had to be altered differently, although, in the end, each fitted the customer.

Another unvarnished truth about patterns is this: a good coat can be produced from almost any pattern which is not radically out of size or shape — provided the tailor knows the art of fitting and altering. *Try-ons or fittings, and alterations just cannot be eliminated from tailoring work, and it is always skill in these departments rather than at pattern drafting, on which success depends.*

The beginner may attempt to draft his patterns, or buy commercial ones, or have them drafted by a tailors' supply house.

Women students, working on normal or near-normal figures, might as well buy the commercial patterns, as these have been tested and are likely to have better seam placements than self-designed ones. Commercial patterns should be purchased one size smaller than marked, as they almost always make up into garments that are too large. This may be due to the operator's failure to sew the seams the required width of ¾ in., or to the manufacturer's practice of purposely designing the patterns large to prevent spoilage through undersized cutting. In any case, if a pattern is large enough (and it is desirable that it be a trifle too large rather than too small) and the coat is being made for a figure not radically out of normal proportions, it is perfectly safe to cut from it, relying on the fitting to bring it down to size, and to correct defects. If ample outlets are left where they are needed, there is no danger of spoiling the goods.

The serious student will, of course, want to draft his own patterns. For difficult forms, it is, indeed, the only thing to do. But he should not expect too much from the pattern, even though well drafted. Nor should he waste time deciding whether to add ¼ in. here or to subtract it there. Let him be content to get the thing pretty nearly right without aspiring after precision where precision is impossible. If he wants perfection in the finished garment, let him concentrate on the fitting and altering, regarding the draft as merely an approximate plan of the coat wanted.

I would counsel all students to draft, if only to understand the taking and applying of measurements in the making of a coat. There are lessons to be learned from drafting that can be learned in no other way.

DRAFTING

The requirements for drafting are: a tailor's square, a piece of wrapping paper longer than the garment by 6 in., and a lead pencil. Tailors ordinarily draft on black paper with chalk, but there is really no great advantage in the use of these over pencil and white paper. The square which is made out of thin wood is very simple to use. It is divided in sections of two-thirds, thirds, sixths and twelfths on the long arm, and in halves, fourths, eighths and sixteenths on the short arm. To give an example of its use: the quantity $\frac{1}{6}$th of 20 in. would be the distance from the elbow of the square to the figure 20 marked in the section of sixths — which would be $3\frac{1}{3}$ in. (Of course, $\frac{1}{6}$th of 20 could be mentally computed as $3\frac{1}{3}$ in., but the purpose of the square is to save the trouble of working fractions in our heads. When, as in the case of a 36-in. chest coat, the scale of 18 in. is easily divisible in halves, thirds and sixths, one could draft without the aid of the notations on the square.)

In drafting, have the base line of your pattern run parallel with the front edge of the bench, so that the top of the pattern is at your right, the bottom at your left.

FIG. 13. Man's semi-fitted coat cut on the formula in this book. This is a good example of the style most men like. The suppression around the waist is moderate, the hips fit rather close, and the shoulders are roomy.

Chapter VII

Coat Making

METHOD OF DRAFTING A MAN'S COAT PATTERN

Coat patterns are generally produced by various formulas, or drafting systems, which utilize half of the chest measure (called the chest scale) to determine all dimensions of the pattern proportionately. An older method of making patterns calls for taking a number of "short measures," as they are called, on the subject and applying them directly to the draft; but often this method does not produce proportionate, or even accurate, patterns for the very figures for which they are designed. The practice most in favor among cutters nowadays is to work from well-proportioned patterns in a range of sizes from, say, a 36 to 48 in. chest, and to alter the pattern as little as possible for any deviation from the normal figure.

In the tailoring trade today, well-designed patterns are best obtained from designers who stock only those models that have been thoroughly tested and proven satisfactory for figures of normal or near-normal proportions. But, given a reliable coat formula, one could also draft his own master pattern in the median size of 40 in. chest and from this original design, produce, by a method called "grading," a whole series of smaller and larger patterns, retaining all the good features of the original.

In this chapter, therefore, I present a formula to produce a perfectly proportioned coat pattern for a subject measuring 40 in. around his chest and about 5 ft. 10 in. in height. The average adult male is close to these proportions.

The student is urged to draft the pattern in the actual size 40 chest and to dimensions given in this formula, and then to grade the pattern into the smaller sizes, 38 and 36, and finally into the larger sizes, 42, 44, and 46. A simple method of grading is taught at the end of this chapter.

I have begun this book with a man's suit coat draft rather than a woman's because it is easier to clothe and fit a male figure. For that very reason, women students of this text, even those who plan to make women's garments exclusively, will do well to study this chapter thoroughly and to make their first coats for male relatives.

The following instructions on the taking of measurements apply to both male and female figures.

Measuring For a Coat

The measurements required to draft a coat are:

HEIGHT OF SUBJECT in inches.

BACK LENGTH OF COAT. Measure from the nape of neck to below round of seat. The nape bone can be felt directly beneath the seam of the shirt collar, and is the most pronounced bump in the spinal column. Measure from slightly above it, in line with the seam of the collar base. A useful formula for a man's coat length is: half of the subject's height (in inches), less 4 in. Let us say that a subject is 5 ft. 4 in. tall, or 64 in. Half of 64 in. is 32 in., and 32 in. minus 4 in. is 28 in., which is the correct coat length for this height.

Women's coat lengths cannot be computed by any such simple rule. With them, it is best to measure one of the subject's old coats whose length is satisfactory. The same recourse is advisable in dealing with all unusually long-bodied or short-bodied subjects of either sex.

WAIST LENGTH. Measure from the nape of neck to the waistline. This measurement is usually ¼ subject's height.

HALF-BACK. Measure from the center-back seam to the right sleeve seam. This measurement is ordinarily ⅙ chest measurement plus 1½ in. on the finished coat. In drafting, it is made ⅓ the chest scale plus 2 in., which includes seams.

41

SLEEVE INSEAM. The length of sleeves is very difficult to predetermine by measuring; and it is only at the try-on stage, when the sleeve is basted in the coat and the pads are in the shoulders, that the tailor is able to fold up the sleeve bottom at exactly the right length. The inseam measurement as taken can be regarded only as an approximation and should be taken a bit long rather than too short.

Now have the subject remove his coat and vest.

CHEST. This measurement, being the most important of them all, must be taken very accurately, for it is by proportionate quantities of one half of the chest measurement that all coats are drafted. One half of the chest, so used, is the "scale."

In taking the chest measurement, be sure that the tape goes over the greatest bulk of the blades at the back, as it has a tendency to slide down in that region; also that it passes across the breasts in male subjects, Fig. 15, but *above* the breasts in females, Fig. 16. Measure over the shirt: neither tight nor loose, but fair.

BREAST (taken only on female subjects). This is much like the chest measure except that the tape is placed directly over the points of the breasts to give an indication of the extra contour that must be provided for them. The usual difference between the chest and breast is 2 to 4 in. For women with full breasts, draft to the chest measure, but open the pattern as in Fig. 20 to introduce space for the breasts.

WAIST. Measure rather loosely around the waist, but this is not a critical measurement in a coat.

SEAT. Measure around the largest part of the buttocks a trifle loosely. Fig. 15.

DEPTH OF ARMHOLE. With unusually short or tall subjects it is often wise to measure the depth of the armhole in the manner shown in Fig. 17. Place a ruler in the armpits and make a chalk mark at A and B. Place the ruler across A-B, locating C. From the nape of the neck to C, plus $\frac{1}{2}$ in. is the depth of the armhole.

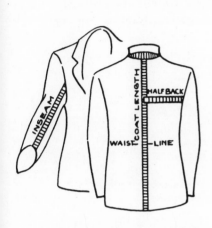

FIG. 14. The four measurements to be taken on the coat.

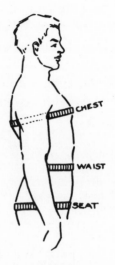

FIG. 15. The three "circular" measurements, chest, waist, and seat.

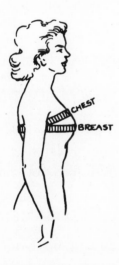

FIG. 16. Showing locations of chest and breast measures on the female figure.

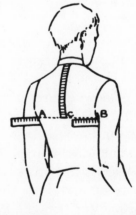

FIG. 17. How to measure the depth of the armhole. Place a ruler in the armpits, and make a chalk mark at A and B. Place ruler across A-B, locating C. From the nape of neck to C, plus ½ in., is the depth of armhole.

Additional remarks on the depth of the armhole are made under "Depth of Armhole," page 48.

Note peculiarities of your subject's build. Is one shoulder lower than the other? Which, and how much? Is his posture normal? Does he stoop? Is he erect? Broad, narrow, or average shoulders?

Decide on style wanted. How many buttons? Back fitted or loose? How wide edge seams?

THE COAT FORMULA

Height in inches, 70 in.	Chest, 40 in.
Coat length, 32 in.	Waist, 35 in.
Waist length, 18 in.	Seat, 40 in.
Half back, plus seams, 9¼ in.	Chest scale, 20 in.
Seams, ¼ in.	Working scale, 24 in.

(Working scale is half chest measure plus 4 in.)

Draw the perpendicular line 1 down to 2, the full coat back length (32 in.).

3 from 1 is ½ chest scale plus ½ in. (10½ in.), or consult the table of armhole depths to locate point 3.

4 from 1 is the waist length, or ¼ height of subject in inches (17½ in.).

5 is midway between 1 and 3.

6 is midway between 1 and 5. Square out from points 1, 2, 3, 4, 5 and 6.

The following are each ¼ working scale (6 in.): 7 from 3; 8 from 7; 9 from 8; and 10 from 9. Square up and down through 10.

11 is midway between 7 and 8. (11 from 3 is 9 in. on this draft, which is the proportionate back width plus two seams.) Square up and down through 11.

12 is midway between 8 and 9. Square up from 12.

13 is midway between 9 and 10.

14 is midway between 9 and 13. Square up from 14, locating point 27.

15 from 10 is 1¼ in., the allowance for lap of front. Square up and down through 15.

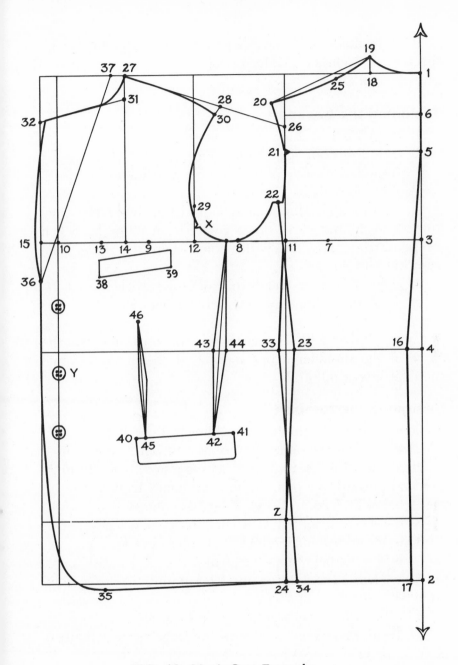

FIG. 18. Man's Coat Formula

45

The scaffolding is now complete, but should be re-checked for accuracy, making certain that all lines are squared truly at right angles.

Designing the backpart

16 from 4 is 1 in. Rule from 5 to 16.

17 from 2 is ¾ in. Rule from 16 to 17.

18 from 1 is $1/6$ scale plus ¼ in. (3¼ in.). Square up to 19.

19 above 18 is ⅞ in. Curve from 19 into 1.

20 is ¾ in. above line 6, and ¾ in. from the vertical line. Rule 19 to 20 and curve down gently from 20 to 21. Notch the pattern at 21, which is the point where the sleeve back seam will join the back.

22 above 11 is 2 in. and ⅜ in. from the vertical line 11-24.

23 is ½ in. inside the same vertical line. Rule 22 to 23 and 23 to 24.

Curve all lines a bit, as suggested in the draft; note that the curve of the shoulder drops about ⅜ in. below the original shoulder line at point 25.

Designing the forepart

26 is ⅝ in. below the horizontal line 6. Rule 26 to 27.

28 from 27 is the same distance as 19 from 20 less ¼ in.

29 above 12 is 1¾ in. Curve, as suggested, from 28 to 29 to 8 and upward to a point ¼ in. horizontally from 22.

30 below 28 is ½ in. Curve 27 to 30 as shown.

X, the sleeve front notch, is 1 in. above chest line.

31 is 1¾ in. below 27 (or $1/12$ scale plus ⅛ in.).

32 is $1/6$ scale below top line of draft.

Rule 31 to 32 and curve into 27, running the curve ¾ in. from 31.

33 is ½ in. from vertical line. Rule 11 to 33.

34 from 24 is 1 in. (or more for large hipped figures). Rule 33 to 34.

35 is ¼ in. below bottom line. Rule 34 to 35.

Center button, Y, is 1 in. below waistline, and the other two buttons are at least 4 in. above and below it.

36 is at least 1 in. above topmost button. (It may be more for a shorter revers.)

37 from 27 is 1 in. Rule from 36 to 37, locating crease of revers and collar.

Curve revers from a point ¼ in. inside 32 down to a point ¼ in. outside 15 and further down into 36. Curve bottom into 35 as suggested.

Locating pockets and darts

38 directly below 13 is 1¾ in. (or 38 is about 4¼ in. from front edge of coat at 36.).

39 from 38 is 4¾ in.; 39 is 1¼ in. below chest line.

Rule 38 to 39 and outline the welt, making its horizontal width 4¾ in. for this size coat (4¼ in. for a 36-chest coat and 5 in. for a 44-chest one). Its vertical finished width is standardly ⅞ in.

40 and 41, the mouth of the side pocket, are usually on the level of the lowest button, or about 9½ in. from coat bottom and parallel with it, i.e., slightly on the slant.

40 from front edge of coat is about 6½ in.

41 from 40 is 6¼ in., the finished width of the mouth of the pocket, as well as of the flap. Vertical width of finished flap is to be 1¾ in.

42 from 41 is 1½ in. Rule from 42 to a point ¾ in. in front of 8.

43 and 44 are ½ in. apart, and this wedge of material is to be cut out.

The front breast suppression dart, 45-46, is often omitted nowadays, and is best omitted for large-waisted figures, although it is desirable for thin-waisted ones. Make point 45 ¾ in. from 40, and line up toward center of breast pocket to a point 3 in. below the welt. It should be almost parallel with coat front edge. Do not cut through this dart, but merely threadmark it and stitch out no more than ⅜ in., tapering sharply into 45 and 46.

DEPTH OF ARMHOLE

The depth of the armhole, 3 from 1, is ½ scale plus ½ in. for normal-shouldered figures whose height is proportionate to their chest size. But in the case of a short person, say 5 ft. 4 in., with a large, 44 in. chest, it would be wrong to make the armhole as deep as ½ scale plus ½ in.; such a deep armhole would make it impossible for the wearer to lift up his arms without also lifting the coat from his shoulders. It would be equally wrong, in the case of a tall lanky person of 6 ft. 2 in. with a small 36 in. chest to make the depth of armhole as shallow as the half-scale; such a shallow armhole would be tight and would cut the subject under the arms. A sloping-shouldered subject, too, would need a deeper armhole than a square-shouldered one of the same height. What must be remembered is that armhole depth is controlled as much by height as by chest size. Therefore, when using the half-scale as the depth determinant seems questionable, either measure the depth of the armhole directly on the subject in the manner demonstrated in Fig. 17, or easier still, consult the following table:

Computing the Depth of Armhole by Chest and Height

		Chests					
	34	36	38	40	42	44	46
5 ft. 4 in.	8¼	8½	8¾	9	9¼	9½	9¾
5 ft. 6 in.	8½	8¾	9	9¼	9½	9¾	10
5 ft. 8 in.	8¾	9	9¼	9½	9¾	10	10¼
5 ft. 10 in.	9	9¼	9½	9¾	10	10¼	10½
6 ft.	9¼	9½	9¾	10	10¼	10½	10¾

(Heights)

Reproduced from *Regal's American Garment Cutter,* by permission of the American Gentleman Publishing Corp., 111 Fifth Ave., New York, N. Y.

In drafting, add ½ in. to the above quantities.

ALTERING THE PATTERN FOR STOOPED AND ERECT FIGURES

The formula as given above will produce a coat very satisfactory in general drape or "balance" for a figure of normal stance, i.e., neither noticeably erect nor stooped. However, when either of these two deviations is apparent, some alteration in the neck and shoulder sections of the normal pattern is necessary. The figures that follow show how this may be done effectively.

Altering the pattern for a stooped figure

Fig. 19 (a). For a slightly stooped or head-forward figure, add ½ in. to the top of the backpart along the neck section and taper down the addition into the point of the shoulder. This may be done by pasting a piece of paper along the top of the pattern, drawing the addition on it, and then cutting on the new outline. (In Figs. 19 and 20, the solid lines are the original pattern, and the dashed lines indicate the changes made.)

Fig. 19(b). On the forepart, cut off a wedge of material ½ in. below the front shoulder point, gradually narrowing the wedge toward and into the shoulder point. Also cut off ½ in. of material below top of revers gradually rounding upward to front shoulder. The solid lines here indicate the original pattern, and the dashed lines show what needs to be cut off.

Note that this alteration simultaneously lengthens the back at the top while shortening the fronts from the top, yet the shoulder and armhole are not affected. If the question is asked why a standard half-inch is recommended rather

FIG. 19(a) Altering the pattern back for stooped posture.
        FIG. 19(b). Altering the pattern forepart for stooped posture.

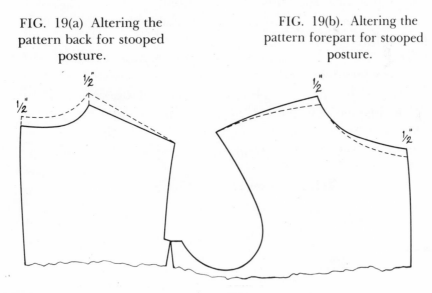

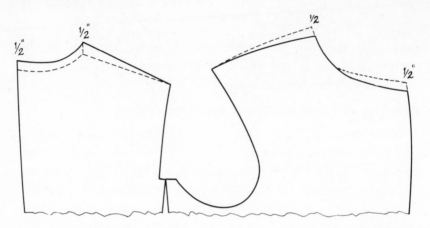

FIG. 20(a). Altering
the pattern back for
erect posture.

FIG. 20(b). Altering
the pattern forepart for
erect posture.

than more or less, the answer is that a moderate change is
favored, and ½ inch is just enough to give the garment the
desired "tendency" suitable for the majority of persons who
stoop or hold their heads forward.

Altering the pattern for an erect figure

Fig. 20(a). For a noticeably erect figure, you need to do
exactly the opposite of what you have done above. Cut away
½ in. of material from the top of the back pattern, gradually
tapering toward the outer shoulder point.

Fig. 20(b). On the forepart you must add ½ in., tapering
the addition into the outer shoulder point, as shown by the
dashed line. Along the top of the revers, you must also add
½ in., tapering into the front shoulder.

Again, by these simple expedients and utilizing a mere
½ in. change, the pattern is made suitable for the general
run of erect figures, without the armhole or shoulder lines
being affected in the least.

THE SLEEVE FORMULA

To be drafted by the chest scale of the coat.
Chest scale, 20 in.
Sleeve inseam, 17 in.
Sleeve bottom, 12 in. around.

50

The topside

Rule the perpendicular line A to B about 24 inches long.

Square out from A to C.

1 below A is ⅓ chest scale plus ¼ in. (7 in. in this draft). Square out horizontally from 1.

2 from 1 is ¼ chest scale. Square out from 2.

3 above 1 is ¾ in. and locates the front notch.

4 from 3 is ½ chest scale (10 in.). Draw the line 3-4.

Square perpendicularly up and down through point 4.

B from 1 is the length of sleeve inseam (17 in. in this case). Square from B to D.

5 is midway between A and C, and 6 midway between 1 and O. Rule from 5 to 6.

7 from A is ⅛ chest scale (2½ in.). Rule from 7 to 3.

Curve from 3 into 5, and down to 4, as shown.

8 from 1 is 1 in.

10 from B is 1 in. Rule from 8 to 10.

X is midway between 8 and 10 and ¾ in. inside line 8-10.

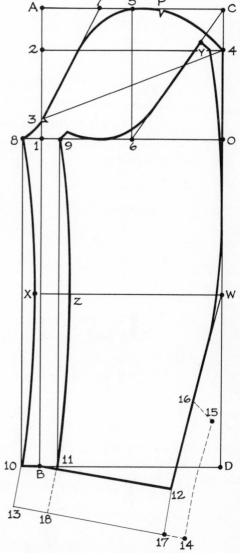

FIG. 21. The Sleeve Formula.

Curve from X up to 8 and down to 10. Curve also from 8 to 3, as shown.

12 from B is the sleeve width measured a bit on the slant (6½ in.).

51

12 is 1¼ in. below the line. Rule from B to 12.

Line X-W is drawn midway between 1 and B and O and D, locating elbow.

Rule from 12 to W, and curve in the elbow ⅜ in. at W, as shown.

P, the notch at the top of the sleeve, is 1½ in. from 5, and indicates the position where the sleeve top is to join the shoulder seam.

The underside

Rule from 6 to C.

9 from 8 is 2¼ in.

11 from 10 is 2¼ in.

Z from X is 2¼ in. Draw the long curve 9-Z-11.

Draw a line from Y, curving a bit above 6 and a little above 9, as shown.

Draw the back line of undersleeve at point Y about ½ in. from 4 and run it down a bit inside O and down into elbow.

The dashed lines at the sleeve bottom indicate the turn-up addition of 2¼ in., which must be added to both top and undersleeves in cutting the cloth. The addition 14-15 is on the undersleeve only and is 1¼ in. from 12-16.

16 above 12 is about 4½ in.

When the draft is finished, cut out the topsleeve, through 13-X-8-3-5-4-0, rounding inside W, then through to 17 and 13.

Lay topsleeve onto another sheet of paper and run a tracing wheel from 18 to 9, around curve above 6, up to Y, then down the curve inside W, and to 16-15-14-18. This will transfer the undersleeve onto the new sheet, which you may then cut out.

This is a very nice sleeve pattern, which should first be drafted in size 40 as here, then graded into smaller and larger sizes. It is not necessary to draft a sleeve for each coat. Once grading is understood, it is possible to cut from this size of sleeve, a set of topsleeves and undersleeves in sizes 36, 38, 42 and 44, or larger, and repeatedly use the same patterns ever after.

PATTERN GRADING

Grading can be defined as the progressive enlargement or reduction of a model pattern in such a way as to retain its proportions in each of the patterns derived from it.

After a tailor or designer has produced and perfected a coat pattern, he will often wish to make a series of smaller and larger patterns, incorporating the original's features and proportions. With the chest-40 pattern shown in Fig. 18, users of this book are provided with an excellent median pattern for doing this.

Grading the forepart

In grading the forepart, Fig. 22(a), first place the pattern forepart on a larger sheet of paper and draw a solid line all around it, A-B-C-D-E-F-G-H, as shown. Next, remove the pattern from the sheet, and rule lines C to X and D to X. Also rule short diagonal lines at G and H and horizontal lines at A, the level of the topmost button, and at B, which is about 7 in. from the bottom. At E, extend the line of the armhole upward a bit.

To *reduce* the pattern to a 39 chest, draw a line ¼ in. *inside* the solid front line at A and B; at all other points, C-D-E-F-G-H, make a mark ⅛ in. inside the solid line. Then, using the forepart pattern as a template, connect the seven points by drawing around the pattern in small sections at a time. You will thus form a new pattern one size smaller all around than the original.

For a two-inch reduction in chest size, draw a line ½ in. inside the front line at A and B; draw all other lines ¼ in. inside the solid outline at points C-D-E-F-G-H. Again, use the original pattern as a template to connect the points and outline the new pattern.

To *increase* the pattern for a 41 chest, draw a line ¼ in. *outside* the solid front line at A and B, but only ⅛ in. outside

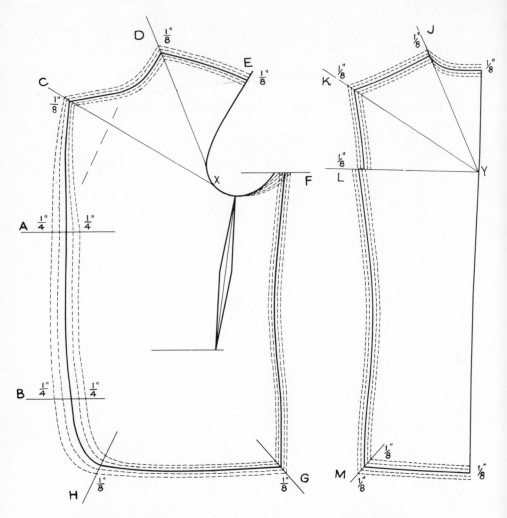

FIG. 22(a). Grading
the forepart.

FIG. 22(b). Grading
the back.

the solid outline at all other points. Again, use the original pattern as a template to connect all points.

The diagram here shows the pattern in five sizes: the original 40-in. chest, shown in solid outline, with sizes 39 and 38 shown inside it in dashed lines, and sizes 41 and 42 shown outside it also in dashed lines.

The main point to remember is that all points increase or decrease only ⅛ in. for each size, except at the front section,

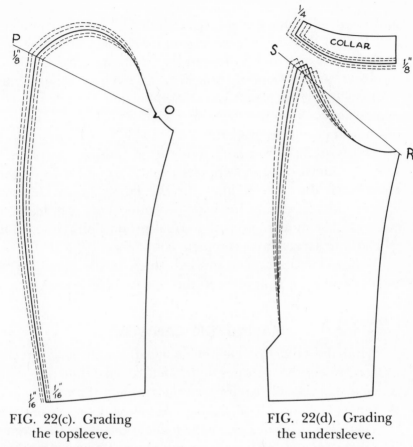

FIG. 22(c). Grading
the topsleeve.

FIG. 22(d). Grading
the undersleeve.

A and B, where the increase or decrease is ¼ in. for each size.

Grading the back

For this process, Fig. 22(b), place the back pattern on a sheet of paper and draw all around it. Rule lines from L to Y, then from K to Y, and finally J to Y. Also, draw a short diagonal line through M. The unit of reduction or enlargement is still the usual ⅛ in. at points J, K, L, M, and at the upper neck and the bottom. The back is used as a template to connect all points.

Grading the sleeve

To grade the sleeve, Figs. 22(c), and 22(d), place the topsleeve and undersleeve patterns on larger sheets of paper and draw all around them. Rule lines O-P on the topsleeve and R-S on the undersleeve. Again make the unit of increase or reduction at P and S the standard ⅛ in. for each size. The topsleeve at the bottom, however, narrows or widens only ¹⁄₁₆ in. for each size. The diagrams are otherwise self-explanatory. (Note the diagram included in Fig. 22(d) showing how the collar is graded.)

Once grading is understood, it is possible to place a size 40 pattern on the cloth, chalk-mark around it, and then chalk-mark the new outlines for the larger or smaller size wanted. In this way, using a single pattern, one can learn to cut coats for most figures of normal proportions from 36 to 44 chest, or larger, with complete confidence.

Women's coats can be graded much in the same way as men's except for a variation in the center front seam.

MAKING THE CANVASES

After the tailor has cut the coat pattern, he may directly proceed to cut the canvases on it, and to make these up. This is a job that should require between two and three hours and that must be done as painstakingly as any of the outer parts of the coat. For the canvases are the foundations of the coat fronts just as the concrete wall is the foundation of a house. It is their function to impart to the coat front a shape similar to that of the wearer. Improperly constructed canvases can ruin an otherwise well-made coat; carefully made ones lend shape and support even to a garment made of flimsy, inferior goods.

Cutting the canvases

"Hairvas" or "hymo" of medium weight are the canvas materials now in use for the general run of sack coats, and either one can be obtained from any tailor's trimming house. Any type of canvas should be shrunk before using, by dipping in cold water and allowing to dry. When cutting the canvases, cut so that their front edge will be on the bias, as this permits any blob in the canvas edge to be shrunk in more easily in the pressing. Fig. 23.

Basting on the haircloth

Haircloth is a stiff material whose woof is made of the manes and tails of horses. It is placed in the upper section of the canvas to keep the breast and the shoulder firm and smooth, and to govern the position of the revers crease. It must always be placed with its selvedge running along the revers crease and about ½ in. inside it. Fig. 24. Tailors who do not use haircloth substitute an extra layer of hymo in the same area.

Cutting the darts

After basting the haircloth onto the canvas, darts must be cut out of it, preferably at the armhole, C, and just below the breast, A, Fig. 24, page 59.

The gorge dart at B is not needed with the coat formula given here, although it is useful in dealing with full-chested figures.

Whichever types of darts are used, as long as they are cut pointing toward the center of the breast, D, Fig. 24, they will fulfill their function properly. Cut the darts through both the canvas and haircloth, making them ⅜ to ½ in. wide at the mouth and gradually narrowing them into sharp points. The darts in the canvas are advantageously made a bit wider and longer than those in the coat. The aim is to put the desired shape in the canvas; the coat will tend to follow that shape.

If a gorge dart is to be used in the canvas, it stands to reason that the coat itself must also have one. But, as I have said, there is seldom any need for the gorge dart if the other two darts are used together.

After the darts are cut out, their edges are machine-sewn together onto strips of silesia, first with a long seam along each side of the dart, then with short zigzags all along it, sealing the raw edges. Fig. 25.

Inserting the shoulder wedge

Remember that while the canvas must be convex or rounded over the breast, it must be made concave in the hollow of the shoulder above. Hollowness of the shoulder section is obtained by cutting down through the center of the shoulder from its top to a depth of about 4 in., and inserting a wedge or V. This wedge, which is cut out of haircloth, is placed between the canvas and haircloth and is sewn to open the shoulder cut 1 in. wide. Its function is to provide room for the large shoulder bone. Along with the wedge it is good practice to insert between the canvas and haircloth a rectangle of linen canvas the width of the shoulder; this is to keep that section stiff and firm so that the finished shoulder will not break or sag. Run a machine stitching along each side of the wedge going through all layers.

Adding the felt, and padding

The next step in canvas construction is to cover the haircloth from top to bottom with a thin layer of cotton felt which is cut somewhat in the shape of the letter U, half of which is laid onto the canvas, the other half meant to be basted onto the backpart and around to the top of the shoulder, Fig. 26. The purpose of this felt is to keep the canvas smooth and to give the coat body over the breast and also around the arm at the back. The entire area covered by the haircloth and felt is now worked over with close rows of loose padding stitches.

Adding body to the front edges

If the canvas is of medium or light weight, it is necessary to sew, along its front edges below the haircloth, a length of wigan for added thickness there. The strip of wigan is cut about 4 in. wide, on the bias, and is laid to cover the bottom edge of the haircloth, extending downward to the coat bottom. It is sewn with about four machine seams running from top to bottom, as shown in Fig. 26.

Sewing on the bridles

Bridles are strips of any unstretchable material (strong sateen sleeve lining cut on the straight will do) 1 in. wide, and as long as the crease of the revers. They are machine-sewn along the crease using a close stitch and drawing them tightly as one goes. One edge is sewn directly over that of the haircloth, the other just outside of it. Thus, the bridle covers the haircloth edge completely, and "stays" the crease so it will not stretch. Indeed, its function is largely to keep the crease short and thus to add to the convexity of the canvas over the breast.

Other ¾ in. strips of lining are then sewn over the remaining raw edges of the haircloth, no part of which must be left uncovered. Finally, the canvas is laid, haircloth side down, on the bench and dry-pressed all over, using very little water on the sponge, and being careful to retain the convex shape of the breast and the hollowness of the shoulder. Fig. 27 depicts the completed canvas.

STEPS IN MAKING THE CANVASES

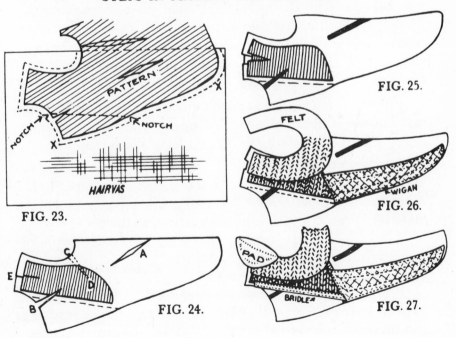

FIG. 23.

FIG. 24.

FIG. 25.

FIG. 26.

FIG. 27.

Steps in making the canvases

Fig. 23. Lay the pattern of the forepart on the hairvas, the pattern front X-X running on the bias of the material. Cut the hairvas about ½ in. outside the pattern all around, notch it at each end of the revers crease, and mark-on the position of the darts with lead pencil. Have the hairvas extend to the center of the armhole narrowing down toward the bottom to about 5 in. wide.

Fig. 24. Cut the haircloth in the shape suggested here, and long enough to reach to the bottom of the revers crease. Baste it on with its selvedge running along the crease line and ½ in. inside of it. Cut out the breast dart, A, and the gorge dart, B. Cut down about 4 in. from E, the mid-shoulder.

Fig. 25. Sew the darts closed onto strips of silesia, stitching in back-and-forth or zigzag fashion. Sew a wedge of haircloth in the center-shoulder cut, opening it 1 in.

Fig. 26. Cut cotton felt in the shape of a large U and baste one end of it onto the haircloth around the armhole section. Work all over the felt and haircloth with rows of padding stitches (downward rows or sidewise ones, it does not matter). Cut a length of wigan on the bias, and machine-sew it onto the lower part of the canvas front, for added thickness.

Fig. 27. Cut a strip of any light unstretchable material, and machine-sew it tightly along the crease edge, one seam covering the edge of the haircloth, the other passing just outside of it.

Beginners who may have difficulty with the extending cotton felt may cut it just outside of the canvas, as in Fig. 27. It is not the best practice, but if the coat is made of substantial material, it can dispense with this felt around the back.

MATCHING AND CUTTING A COAT

Before cutting out a coat (or a whole suit) lay out all the parts of your pattern on the cloth as close together as possible, and mark around each of them with chalk. Do not, like many

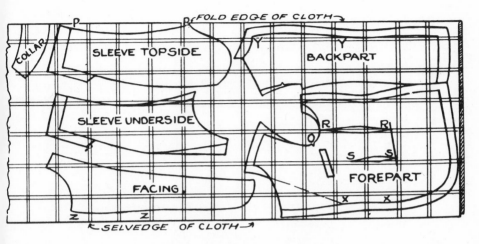

FIG. 28. Matching and cutting.

beginners, cut the parts only as they are needed, as you will waste some of your cloth and possibly end up without sufficient material to get out all the parts.

The diagram, Fig. 28, shows the positions in which to lay out the parts in striped or checked goods. (It is not meant to suggest such a layout from the viewpoint of economizing on cloth, since, to that end, the parts should be placed as close to one another as possible.)

Note that the bottoms of the foreparts and backparts are on the same line, to insure the matching of the checks at the side seams. The front at X-X should run perfectly parallel with the stripe of the cloth. The back at Y-Y should do the same. The facing should follow the stripe at Z-Z, and the sleeve topside at P-P. Sleeves should be placed so that the horizontal stripe or check matches with that of the forepart above O, the notch.

Begin by chalk-lining around the forepart of the pattern, allowing inlays as suggested. Then outline the backpart. All inlays have an important function. Omit none.

Cut out the underarm dart at R-R, but do not cut out the breast dart S-S nor the mouth of the pocket.

The outside collar is to match at the back of the neck; it is impossible to control the match at the front where the collar

61

joins the revers. Nor can we control the match in the shoulder seam. The outside collar is cut on the fold of the cloth, as shown.

Having cut the coat, make chalk marks on the wrong side of all the parts, as, with some cloths, it is very easy to mistake the wrong side for the right.

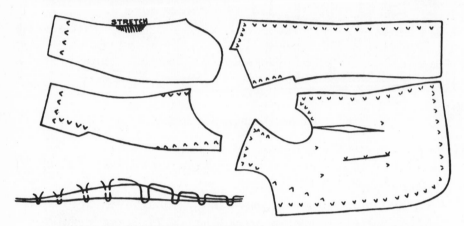

FIG. 29. Threadmarking. The marking thread is passed in the manner of a wide basting stitch through both layers of cloth. Then the stitches are cut from the top, and finally between the layers. Side view of the operation is shown in lower left diagram.

Threadmarking

A coat cannot be accurately made up unless each of its parts are marked on both sides with coarse cotton thread in the manner shown in Fig. 29. Immediately after cutting, while the parts lie together, marking thread must be passed along all the inlays, the crease of revers, the mouths of the pockets and the front breast dart. The position of the buttons must also be marked. Pass the marking thread in the manner of a wide basting stitch through both layers of cloth, then cut the stitches from the top, and finally between the layers. The side view of the operation is shown in the lower left diagram, Fig. 29.

Stretching

Tailors of the old school did a good deal of stretching and

shrinking of various areas in making their coats, but modern methods of cutting aim at producing garments that go together naturally and with a minimum of manipulation. The only part that needs to be stretched is the hollow of the sleeve topside, Fig. 29. Put a little moisture on this area, and as you apply the hot iron with your right hand, stretch gently with your left. Do not stretch too much; $\frac{3}{16}$ in. is usually ample.

BASTING THE COAT FOR THE TRY-ON

After the canvases have been made, the tailor sets about preparing the coat for the first try-on. An experienced craftsman, when he is pretty certain that his pattern was correct, will generally build in the two side pockets and the outside breast pocket, baste the foreparts onto the canvases, join the foreparts to the back, and baste on the sleeves and the collar. When he is through, the coat will look a good deal, in its outlines, like the finished garment.

This bold procedure, however, is for the experienced only; the beginner had best do as few things as possible to the coat before trying it on the client. For the time being, he should forget all about the pockets, the sleeves and the collar, and concern himself solely with the body part of the coat. Fundamentally, the purpose of the try-on is to see if the coat body hangs or "balances" properly, is of the correct size and length, and has the correct shoulder width and slope. When the coat body has been made right, one can handle the problems of the pockets, sleeves, and collar, with more confidence.

Sewing the darts

Sew, first, all the darts in the foreparts: the long underarm dart, the breast dart, the gorge dart if any, and the center-shoulder dart if the coat is cut as in Fig. 20. In custom tailoring, all seams are sewn $\frac{1}{4}$ in. wide; this is standard. (If you sew your seams $\frac{3}{8}$ in. wide, you will decrease the size of your coat by over 1 in.) In sewing a dart, have its end decrease very gradually into a sharp point, as any too sudden decrease will

63

result in blobbing of the cloth below the point. After seaming, dry-press the area around the points thoroughly, shrinking in with a little moisture.

BASTING COAT FOR THE TRY-ON

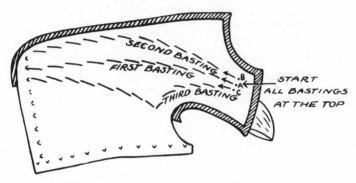

FIG. 30. Lay the forepart on the canvas interlining, and baste down from A to the bottom of the coat. Baste down from B in like manner. Finally from C.

Basting in the canvases

Next, baste the foreparts onto the canvases, Fig. 30. All bastings must start from a point about 2 in. from the top of the shoulder, and it is important that the starting points, A, B and C, be only about ¾ in. apart. When the bastings are too close to the edges, the tailor is hindered in taking the seams and in fastening the pads. The relative positions of the bastings as suggested in Fig. 30 are quite accurate. Place the left canvas, haircloth side down, on the bench, and lay on it the left forepart right side up. The first basting must be run down the center of the canvas, the tailor smoothing the cloth downward with a good deal of care as he bastes. The second basting, beginning at B, is run just inside and along the revers crease, and along the front of the coat about 1¼ in. inside the edge. The third basting, C, is run around the armhole about 2 in. inside its edge, and turns at the armhole base, following the inside edge of the canvas toward the bottom. The right forepart of the coat is basted in the same way, beginning at the top.

64

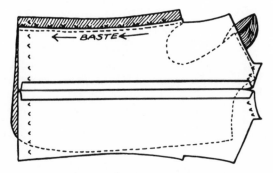

FIG. 31. Baste the backpart onto the forepart, the backpart edge following the threadmarks on the forepart.

Basting the back to the foreparts

Now, lay the backparts, as cut and threadmarked, on the
bench. Baste them one onto the other, down the center back
barely inside the threadmarks, being very careful that any
horizontal checks in the material match perfectly. Even a
slight error in the matching of the cloth in this seam will be
very noticeable, and must be avoided. Machine-sew the backs
together beginning the seam at the top and running it ¼ in.
inside the threadmarks. Press open the seam. Now, lay the
right forepart right side up on the bench, and lay the backpart
on it, right side down, as shown in Fig. 31. The edge of the
back should be placed along the threadmarks, and basted from
the notch of the armhole down to the bottom of the coat. Proceed to baste the back onto the left forepart in the same way.

Basting the shoulders

Now, fold the coat inside out laying the right shoulder of
the backpart along the threadmarks of the shoulder of the right
forepart. Baste from the neck to the shoulder end as shown in
Fig. 32. Remember that the shoulder of the backpart is ³⁄₁₆ in.
wider than that of the forepart, and this extra width must be
fulled on carefully in basting. Baste the left shoulder in the
same way as the right.

Baste the revers from the canvas side with a wide padding
stitch, meanwhile rolling them in the manner shown in Fig. 88.

Turn in all inlays along the fronts and bottom of the coat, basting them ¼ in. inside the threadmarks.

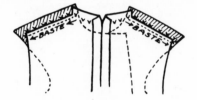

FIG. 32. Baste backpart shoulders onto shoulders of foreparts, as shown. Remember that the backpart shoulder is ¼ in. wider than that of the forepart, and this extra width must be fulled on evenly.

Padding the shoulders

The function of padding is to give the shoulders a substantial, athletic appearance which is stylish nowadays in both men's and women's wear. But heavy padding is a mistake where an individual is square-shouldered in the first place.

For persons with sloping shoulders, padding is a great aid in imparting a more normal appearance, as long as it is placed squarely on top of the shoulder and is well tapered or graduated so that its outlines do not show through the coat.

In persons with one shoulder slightly lower than the other, the insertion of an extra pad in the lower side often completely corrects the defect in the hanging of the coat.

Pads should be basted in the shoulders of the coat only after these have been basted closed for the try-on. The pads are basted to and *under* the canvas, so that they are in direct contact with the shoulder, and half of them should normally extend beyond the canvas toward the back of the armscye.

The tailor may purchase his pads ready-made at a few cents a pair, or he may make them himself by packing cotton wadding between two semicircular layers of thin felt, passing a number of wide, loose basting stitches through the whole. The main care is that the pad be "graduated" so that the thick outside edge will gradually taper into a very thin layer. Such pads are about 6½ in. long by 4 in. wide. Their thickest part, pressed down, should be ½ in. thick.

Finally, press all seams from the inside of the coat, lapping them to one side so that they will not bunch during the try-on.

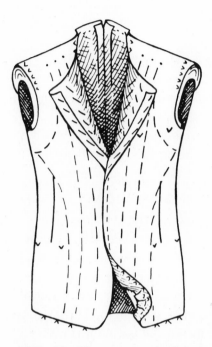

FIG. 33. The coat ready for the first try-on. Note that the center-back seam is left unsewn above the neckline. This is to prevent constriction at the back neck during the fitting.

The body of the coat now appears as illustrated in Fig. 33, and is ready to try on the subject.

FITTING — THE FIRST TRY-ON

Fitting may be defined as the technique of correcting defects in an unfinished garment while it is being tried on by its intended wearer. It is the hardest thing to learn in the entire field of tailoring, and the most important, for it is at the try-on stage that the mistakes made in the previous measuring of the subject and in the drafting of his pattern must be corrected. Fitting, in short, is the climax in the making up of a custom-made garment, and every tailor who has ever made a name for himself has owed his success to proficiency in this art.

What is the procedure in fitting? The novice, baffled when he tries on his first coat, not knowing where to start his correcting, is bound to ask many questions. I can only answer by giving my own system, for, in this operation, every tailor develops his own individual routine.

In my practice I use two or three try-ons, and I think three is none too many with difficult subjects.

At the first try-on, I aim at correcting only the body of the coat, ignoring completely the sleeves and the collar. I proceed to check carefully — very carefully — on each of seven points, in the order given.

(1) Is the balance of the coat right? That is, does the coat

hang well, with the fronts perpendicular and also parallel?

(2) Is the shoulder capacity right? Is the run of the armhole right?

(3) Is the coat size right? Is it too large, or too small?

(4) Is the coat length right?

(5) Mark the run of the collar base, and determine the length of the crease edge of the collar.

(6) Mark the sleeve pitch at the wrist.

(7) Are the pockets and buttons in the right places?

Let us consider further each of these seven points.

(1) BALANCE AND HANG OF FRONTS

If the coat is properly drafted and the balance right, its fronts will hang side by side almost perpendicularly when it is tried on. It is to be expected that the space between them will be a trifle wider at the waist than at the chest, because of the unfinished condition of the edges; but the fronts will neither gape wide open at the bottom nor crisscross there. If they show a tendency to do either, the balance of the garment is faulty.

Fronts too long in relation to the back

A coat whose fronts gape open and whose back leaves the seat at the bottom, will also show a tendency to leave the neck at the back when the fronts are pinned closed, Figs. 34, 35. These defects are seen to occur in garments worn by stooping, round-shouldered, forward-headed persons. The reason for them is that the fronts are too long at the top. You may easily determine how much too long they are by pinning out a horizontal fold just below the shoulder seam, Fig. 36. This pinned-out fold will cause the front edges of the coat to fall at once in their more natural, perpendicular position.

You can remedy the defect, of course, by cutting out the strip of excess cloth from the top shoulder of the forepart, Fig. 37. But as this method necessitates scooping the armhole, and cutting from the top of the revers, most tailors prefer to use another means of attaining the same end. They "slide" up the back on the side seams, thus lengthening the back and estab-

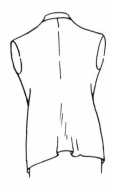

FIG. 34.   FIG. 35.

FIGS. 34, 35. Fronts too long in relation to back. Coat gapes at front, leaves the seat at back.

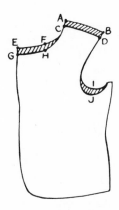

FIG. 36.   FIG. 37.

FIG. 36. The extent of the defect determined by pinning out a fold across the front shoulder. This lifts up the fronts to their normal position by shortening them from the top. FIG. 37. One method of altering for the defect. Lower the shoulder seam from A-B to C-D, removing the shaded portion. To the same extent lower the top of the revers, as from E-F to G-H; and deepen the armhole from I to J

69

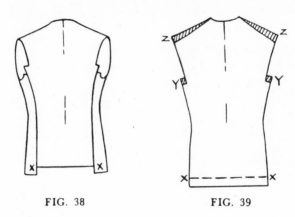

FIG. 38   FIG. 39

FIG. 38. Another, often preferred, method of correcting the defect: sliding up the back on the side seams, in fitting. FIG. 39. Alterations necessitated by sliding up the back. The coat must be lengthened below X-X, the notches lowered at Y, and the shoulders sloped by cutting off wedges at Z.

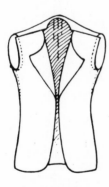

FIG. 40

FIG. 40. The defect partially corrected by shifting the forepart shoulders outwardly. This recourse, however, throws excess material to the front of the arm and under it, and it is necessary to cut some away where shown by the dashed line.

lishing its harmony with the fronts, Figs. 38, 39. This method does not decrease the depth of the armhole or disturb the position of the revers, the only changes required being that the back be lengthened at the bottom below X-X, the armhole notches lowered at Y-Y, and the shoulders sloped by cutting off wedges at Z-Z.

If raising the back in this manner does not completely remedy the gaping of the fronts, and they still refuse to fall in almost parallel lines, the trouble may be due to a faulty shoulder seam. In such a case, the shoulder seam is unbasted, and the shoulder of the forepart is shifted outward (away from the neck of the wearer), thus exerting a straightening effect on the fronts, Fig. 40. This recourse, however, often throws excess material to the front of the arm and under it, and it is necessary to cut some away where shown by the dashed lines in Fig. 40. Generally the strip cut from the front of the hole is no more than ½ in. at the widest, and the underarm seam must be taken in to the same extent. This alteration, called "scooping the front of scye," is often required for subjects having forward shoulders, or who are poorly fleshed under the arms.

DEFECTS OF BALANCE, Problem 2

FIG. 41.   FIG. 42.

FIGS. 41, 42. Fronts too short in relation to back. Coat fronts crisscross; folds gather over the seat at the back. (*Cont. on p. 72*)

Fronts too short in relation to the back

When the coat fronts crisscross at the bottom, the back of the coat also shows a tendency to gather or break over the seat in horizontal folds, Figs. 41, 42. This trouble, which is very common with erect subjects, indicates that the back is too long at the top. The excess length can be determined exactly by pinning out a horizontal fold across the upper back, Fig. 43.

The defect is commonly remedied by sliding down the back on the side seams, to the extent determined by the pinned fold.

71

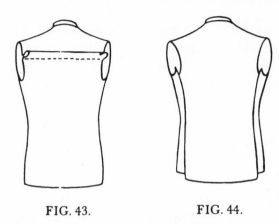

FIG. 43.   FIG. 44.

FIG. 43. The extent of the defect is determined by pinning out the fold of excess across the back. FIG. 44. Best method of altering. Back is slid down on the side seams, and the excess length cut away at the bottom.

This shortens the back at the top, and its excess length passes to the bottom where it is cut off, Fig. 44.

While the work of correcting faulty balance, or hang, can be done by merely sliding the back up or down on the side seams, it can also be done by taking up or letting down the foreparts at the shoulder seams. And so, while the beginner, in his study of fitting, may confine himself to manipulating the back, later he ought to learn to obtain the same effects by manipulating the fronts. In the matter of balance, there are two ways of attaining the same end.

As soon as I have noted the hang of the coat fronts with an eye as to their balance, I lap the fronts evenly as they will be when finished and buttoned, and pin them together that way. I always avoid cutting the fronts slightly on the skew to remedy defects of balance; for though this may be resorted to in plain goods, it is extremely objectionable practice in striped or checked materials where the stripe must be kept parallel with the edge of the front.

All this playing around with the balances is the most important part of fitting, and I urge the beginner to experiment at great length with the sliding of the back up and down, and with the shifting of the neckpoint of the forepart inward and outward. A tailor's dummy is useful for these experiments.

At no time try to force cloth to lie otherwise than it has a mind to. If your fronts must be pulled to close correctly and refuse to fall in the proper position, you need to correct something, and no amount of pulling, stretching, shrinking or ironing will attain your ends.

Sometimes you will want to add cloth at the fronts; sometimes you will want to pare some away. In such cases, pin the fronts in the position they naturally tend to fall on one another and draw a chalkline along the edge of the overlapping front onto the other. In men's coats, the line will be drawn on the right front following the edge of the left one; in the women's coat, the line will be on the left front. This line is most important because it is the only guide you will have in trimming the edges and determining the width of the lap. Even after the fronts have been made up and the coat is about to be pressed, this line is marked through with a thread (the chalk being brushed away to avoid its sticking to the cloth in pressing) for it will finally serve as a guide in sewing the buttons in their proper positions.

(2) SHOULDER CAPACITY

Having corrected the balance of the coat, the tailor passes to the consideration of shoulder capacity.

If the coat has been well planned, it should preferably be a trifle roomy in the shoulders, to provide room for padding as well as to make it easier to determine how much should be taken out (for it is always easier to fit by reducing sections than by adding to them). Excess shoulder room, or capacity, has no effect on the balance of the garment, as a coat balances independently of the cloth covering the shoulder ends. Therefore, as long as there is plenty of room there, the tailor can attend to the problems of balance without obstacle. But if the coat shoulder slopes too much, the entire neck section is lifted up by the shoulder ends, and fitting cannot be accomplished without ripping the shoulder seams at their outer ends.

Shoulder capacity has to be determined precisely if the coat is to look well. A little too much results in wrinkles back of the arms, while too little causes the collar to lift from the neck. Square-shouldered or normal-shouldered subjects give less trouble in adjustment than sloping-shouldered ones on whom the coat shoulders frequently tend to sag no matter how much is taken out. Nor, with such types, does added padding lift the shoulders adequately; only as much padding can be placed in a coat shoulder as can be packed directly on top of the shoulder, and never must the pads extend far to the front or the back of the shoulder where they will bunch uncomfortably.

Having pinned out the excess cloth covering the shoulders, the tailor should mark the run of the seam around the armhole with a well-sharpened piece of chalk. Frequently, the armhole will have to be "scooped" at the front; sometimes, clear up to the top of shoulder. Occasionally, it will have to be deepened at the base. But, whatever you do, do not, at this stage, cut out all that appears to be excessive, but wait until you have basted in the sleeves, tried on the coat, and know how much you can dispense with.

(3) COAT SIZE

The tailor may now turn to the adjustment of the coat size, which is of course done mainly at the side seams, though cutting from, or adding to, the fronts may also be resorted to when necessary. Here again, it is easier for the tailor if the coat is slightly on the large side, for then, by merely pinning the excess in a fold along each side seam, he can determine exactly how much needs to be taken out there. If the coat is too small, it is much more difficult to determine the amount it should be enlarged. One can only approximate, then. Of course, reducing at the side seams has some effect on the upper back, which must be also narrowed along the armhole. If the back is of the proper width, however, the reduction should be done from the foreparts only.

(4) COAT LENGTH

Some rules relating to the proper length of coats have been given in the section on measuring, but the length of coats is largely governed by individual taste. Usually, a tailored coat is designed to cover the buttocks completely, that is, it extends to the point where the buttocks break into the thighs. No precise rule can be given outside of that. The tailor simply marks all around the coat bottom where he judges it should be shortened. This he does with a yardstick, measuring from the floor. Then he turns up and pins the bottom all around so that the client may judge for himself if that length is agreeable.

(5) THE COLLAR

The tailor now chalks the run of the collar base seam all around the neck of the coat at the back. This marking should follow the line of the base of the shirt collar there. Of course, it is important mainly when the original seam line has been thrown out of place by corrections of defective balances. Then, with the tape, the tailor measures the length of the collar crease from the top of the left revers, at the break, around the back to the top of the right revers. This measurement will enable him to cut the collar exactly the right length.

(6) SLEEVE PITCH

Most sleeves are pitched to hang with the fronts of their bottoms in line with the center of the mouth of the side pocket. However, to this rule, there are exceptions. Stooped persons carry their arms forward; erect persons carry them backward. Consequently, the tailor asks his client to stand with arms falling normally at the sides, and makes a mark on the coat in front of each wrist. This mark will later serve as a guide in basting the sleeves at the proper pitch. The coat must be pinned closed at the front when making this mark.

(7) POCKET AND BUTTON POSITION

Experienced craftsmen often construct their coat pockets

before the first try-on of the coat, but the beginner is wiser if he merely chalks the outline of the pocket flaps on the foreparts. In this way, he may judge at the time of the try-on if the pockets will look right where he plans to put them.

The same practice is advisable in determining the position of the buttons.

This completes the operations for the first try-on.

Altering and re-marking

Immediately, while the needed changes are still fresh in his mind, the tailor re-marks with chalk and with marking thread the parts which need altering. This done, he rips the shoulders apart, and rips the foreparts from the back; or he may immediately sew up the side seams on the machine, thus keeping the coat in one piece from the beginning. Having the coat in one piece makes it a bit unwieldy for building-in the pockets, but the job can be done easily enough that way, and is, I think, the best method for beginners.

Trimming the fronts

Next, the tailor unbastes the turn-ins along the fronts and bottom and presses them flat. He lays one forepart onto the other, the canvases lying between, and bastes the front edges in perfect congruence. Very carefully, he marks the run of the front edges and the bottom, being especially careful about the shape of the revers and the round of the bottom. Then he cuts through both foreparts and canvases at the same time, from the round of the bottom to the notch of the lapel.

He may then rip out the canvases preparatory to making the pockets.

It is at this stage, too, that he interrupts his work on the coat to correct the pattern. Later, should he wish to make another coat for the same client, this corrected pattern will considerably facilitate the task.

MAKING THE POCKETS

Because beginners find it difficult to locate their pockets properly, and a misplaced pocket can very seriously mar the appearance of a coat front, it is advocated here that pockets be constructed after the first try-on. This course necessitates ripping out the canvases after the try-on and rebasting them to the foreparts after the pockets are made, but the extra work is preferable to placing the pockets wrongly. When one has gained experience, one can save time by constructing all pockets directly after cutting the coat.

The ordinary coat has three types of pockets. At the sides are "flapped" pockets; at the left breast, a "welt" pocket; and inside the coat, over the right breast (in a man's coat), a "piped" pocket built into the lining. In a woman's coat, this inside breast pocket may be omitted. Step-by-step instructions for making the three kinds of pockets are given in Figs. 48 to 84.

Staying the pockets

Having marked the pocket mouths, lay the coat foreparts wrong side up on the bench. Take some wigan, or any thin

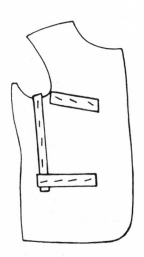

piece of unstretchable material and cut, on the straight of it, three strips 1½ in. wide by 7½ in. long. Baste one of these, on the reverse side of coat, across the mouth of each of the three pockets. They will act as stays to prevent stretching. Fig. 45.

Next, cut two strips of wigan about 13 in. long and 1 in. wide, and baste one of them from the back end of the mouth of each pocket up to the base of the armhole. The function of these strips is to suspend the back end of the pocket from the

FIG. 45. Staying the pockets with strips of wigan.

armhole seam. The front end of the pocket is supported by the canvas, to which it is firmly tacked.

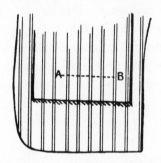 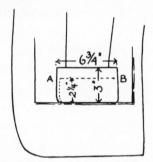

FIG. 46. Matching the flaps. Piece of cloth is laid to match, and the mouth of the pocket, A-B reproduced on piece.

FIG. 47. Dimensions of flap as designed on line A-B and ready to be cut out.

MAKING THE SIDE POCKETS

Cutting the flaps

Cutting flaps is simple enough in plain goods, but a bit difficult in striped or checked materials.

Fig. 46 demonstrates how to lay a piece of cloth, right side up, on the coat front, directly over the region where the flap will be in the finished garment. The pattern of the piece must be matched directly upon that of the coat, and the line of the pocket mouth (A-B) reproduced on the piece.

Fig. 47 shows the dimensions and shape in which to cut the flap. Quantities given include seam allowances for a 6¼-in. flap.

Preparing the silesias

Fig. 48. Cut two pieces of silesia 7½ x 17½ in. (for man's coat) 6½ x 16½ in. (for woman's). Cut also, from the same cloth as the coat, and on the length of the cloth, two facings 7½ x 2 in.

Fig. 49. Machine-sew ends of silesias onto the facings, making the overall length 19 in.

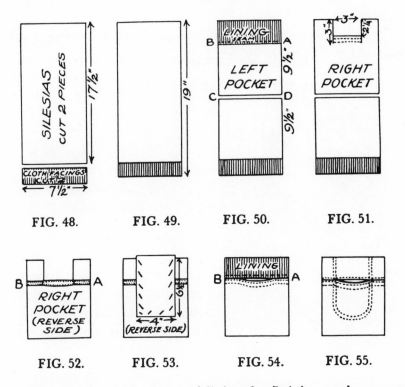

FIG. 48.   FIG. 49.   FIG. 50.   FIG. 51.

FIG. 52.   FIG. 53.   FIG. 54.   FIG. 55.

Fig. 50. Cut two pieces of lining 3 x 7½ in., and sew one of these over the top end of the *left* pocket, as from A to B. Divide and cut the silesia at its center, C-D, resulting in two pieces, 9½ x 7½ in.

Fig. 51. A small inside pocket, sometimes called a "change pocket" must now be built in the right pocket. Make two cuts 3 in. apart and 3 in. deep, as shown, leaving a ¾ in. "tongue" extending between the cuts.

Fig. 52. Cut a length of staytape, 7½ in. long. Turn the pocket to the reverse side, fold the tongue around the staytape, and sew a seam along both edges of the tape and through the tongue.

Fig. 53. Cut a 6½ x 4 in. piece of silesia and baste it on to the reverse side of the pocket.

Fig. 54. Now, turn the pocket to the right side again and sew on the other lining piece, as from A to B, flush with the mouth of the change pocket.

Fig. 55. Sew two "horseshoe" seams through lining and silesia, to form a pocket 3½ in. deep.

MAKING THE SIDE POCKETS

Fig. 56. Lay a piece of lining, right side up, on the bench. Baste flaps right side down and on the bias, on the lining.

Fig. 57. Trim lining around the flaps, and seam around three sides, the flaps being laid lining side up on the machine.

Fig. 58. Turn flaps right side out, basting around the edges.

Fig. 59. Sew a close finish seam around the flap edge, remove bastings and press. Draw a chalk line 2⅛ in. inside finished edge.

Fig. 60. Lay flap, lining side up, on coat forepart, basting chalk line of flap onto chalk line on coat. Seam through the chalk line, fastening both ends securely with back-and-forth stitches.

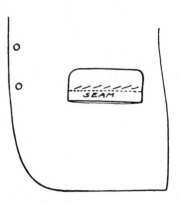

Fig. 61. Seam silesia facing ¼ in. below flap seam, both seams being of the same length.

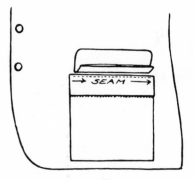

Fig. 62. Cut between the two seams, from the reverse of the coat.

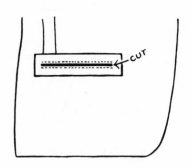

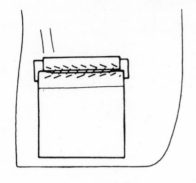

Fig. 63. Turn in pocket and top of flap through the cut, and baste turned edges into position from the outside. This figure shows pocket from the inside of coat, following this operation. Close the pocket mouth with a loose basting.

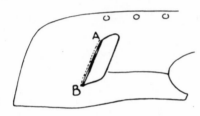

Fig. 64. Sew a finish seam along lower edge of pocket mouth, A to B. Leave the thread ends long, at both ends, so that they may be drawn through and tied from the inside.

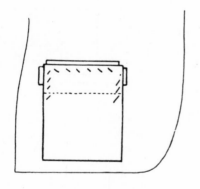

Fig. 65. Turning again to inside of coat, baste-on the silesia backpart of the pocket, as shown. The silesia with the small change pocket goes on the right side.

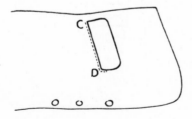

Fig. 66. Seam from the outside from C to D, going around the corners about ¼ in. Again, leave the thread ends long, and draw them through.

Fig. 67. Lifting the coat out of the way, sew around the entire pocket, and trim it even. Finish with a bar-tack at each end of pocket mouth.

MAKING THE OUTSIDE BREAST POCKET

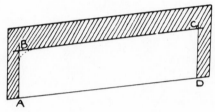

Fig. 68. The welt is matched in the same way as is the flap. It is marked on the right side of the cloth, to the dimensions that follow: B from A, and C from D, are $1\frac{1}{8}$ in. D from A is $4\frac{1}{2}$ in. for man's coat of average size; about 4 in. for woman's coat. Top line is $\frac{1}{2}$ in. above B-C. End lines are $\frac{1}{4}$ in. outside A-B and C-D.

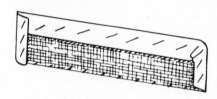

Fig. 69. Cut a strip of wigan on the straight of material, $1\frac{1}{8}$ in. wide and to the shape and length of the finished welt, A-B-C-D. Baste this onto the reverse side of the welt, where it will act as a stay. Overcast wigan to welt along the bottom edge; then turn in the seams all around, on lines A-B, B-C, and C-D, basting carefully for straight edges and folding the front corner in a small curve. Finally, run a narrow finish seam all around the edges, and press.

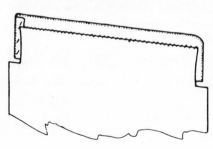

Fig. 70. Cut two pieces of silesia, $5\frac{1}{2}$ x $6\frac{1}{2}$ in. in size, with the narrow ends on the slant in keeping with the slant of the welt. Hand-sew one of these pieces onto the welt; then nick out the ends, as illustrated.

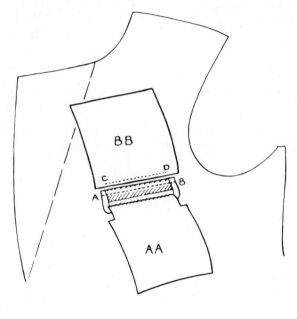

FIG. 71.

Fig. 71. Baste welt to coat at A-B, and seam. Seam other piece of silesia, as at C to D.

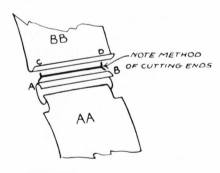

FIG. 72.

Fig. 72. Cut between the seams as illustrated by the black line. The nicks pointing toward the corners of the welts are diagonal; those cut upward vertically are $\frac{1}{4}$ in. inside edge of welt, A and B.

Draw the silesia, AA (but not the welt proper) through the cut to the inside of the coat. From the inside, press open the seam, A-B. Draw also the silesia, BB, inside the coat and press it congruent onto AA.

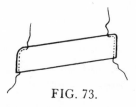

FIG. 73.

Fig. 73. Turning now to the outside of the coat, baste down the welt, and sew both of its ends on the machine, as shown, leaving the thread ends long.

Then draw the thread ends through, and tie them from the inside. Securely tack pocket ends from the inside of the coat with an invisible tack. Sew around the silesias, completing the pocket.

Attaching the facings to the linings

Having made the outside pockets, the tailor now turns to the preparation of the facings. This involves (1) sewing the facings to the linings, and (2) making the inside breast pocket.

Cutting the forepart lining properly is important and may be done in the following manner:

Place the facing on the pattern of the forepart and draw a line on the pattern $\frac{1}{2}$ in. inside the edge of the facing. This will be the dotted line, U-V, and should be perforated with small holes.

Lay out the lining, folded lengthwise, on the bench, and on it lay part of pattern, U-V-W-X-Y. Leave outlets of at least 1 in. all around except beyond the line U-V, where no further seam allowance should be made. Cut out the underarm dart,

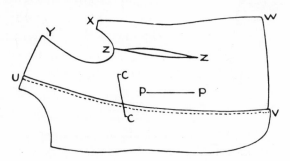

FIG. 74. Attaching facings to linings.

Z-Z, but the breast dart, P-P, need not be cut but only marked with chalk.

(At this point, while you have the lining on the bench, cut out the lining for the back of the coat and for the top and undersides of the sleeves. Cut each of those parts 2 in. longer than the pattern, at the bottom. Lay them aside for future use.)

Now, baste the forepart linings to the facings, as along U-V, and sew them together on the machine. Also, sew the under-arm and breast darts, and press the whole.

Take the facing of the right forepart and mark pocket mouth as at C-C. It is marked about 1½ in. below the level of the armhole base, and should cut into the facing about ¾ in. Its total width to be 5¼ in.

Making the inside breast pocket

The diagrams 75, 76, 80, and 83 depict the facing from the reverse side. Diagrams 77, 78, 79, 81, and 84 show the facing from the outside. The dashed line in Fig. 75 marks the run of the pocket mouth.

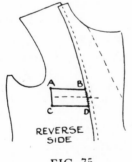

REVERSE SIDE

FIG. 75.

Fig. 75. Cut a small rectangular piece of the same cloth as the coat (A-B-C-D), and sew it flush to the edge of the facing at B-D. It will function as a base, giving body to the edge of the pocket.

Fig. 76. Cut a piece of wigan about 8 in. long, and baste it across mouth of pocket and over edge of facing. It will function as a stay.

86

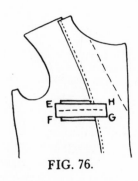

FIG. 76.

FIG. 77.

Fig. 77. Turn facing over to the right side, and baste across the mouth of the pocket a rectangle of lining, its right side facing downward. Reproduce the line of the pocket mouth onto this lining piece.

FIG. 78.

Fig. 78. Sew around the line so drawn a continous seam in the shape of an elongated rectangle, $\frac{3}{8}$ in. wide and $5\frac{1}{4}$ in. long. Cut lengthwise between the seams, nicking diagonally toward the corners at both ends.

FIG. 79.

Fig. 79. Turn in the lining piece through the cut, basting it into two piped edges. Then baste the mouth of pocket closed, as shown, and press the whole from the reverse.

FIG. 80.

FIG. 81.

Fig. 80. Cut two pieces of silesia, 6¼ x 8 in., their top edges being slanted to agree with the slant of breast pocket. Baste one of these, AA, onto the reverse side of the facing, as illustrated.

Fig. 81. Lay facing, right side up, on the machine, and seam from H to I, joining silesia AA to pocket. Fold the silesia downward and press.

FIG. 82.

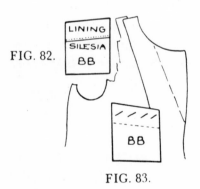

FIG. 83.

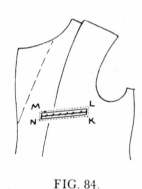

FIG. 84.

Fig. 82. Face top of remaining silesia, BB, with a piece of lining.

Fig. 83. Baste silesia BB congruent on AA.

Fig. 84. Again lay facing on the machine, right side up, and seam around top piping from K to L to M to N. Stitch the ends back and forth to form a tack. Sew around the edges of the silesias, forming the pocket.

MAKING THE FRONTS

For clarity's sake, the *right* front, exclusively, is illustrated in this series.

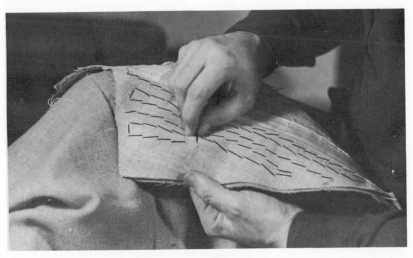

FIG. 85. Padding the revers.

Fig. 85. After the pockets have been made, and pressed from the inside, rebaste the canvases to the foreparts just as they were before being ripped off. Next, pad the revers, making the stitches close but not tight. Start padding in up-and-down rows along the bridle edge, rolling the canvas onto the revers with the left hand. The roll is most important, as it will be a permanent feature of the finished coat.

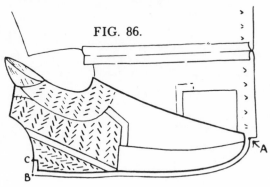

FIG. 86.

Fig. 86. Pare away the canvases ¼ in. or a bit more inside the edge of the fronts, from the round of the bottom, at A, up to the corner of the revers and 2 in. inside the corner at B, to C. (In women's coats, reduce this 2 in. to 1¾ in.)

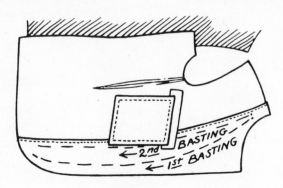

FIG. 87.

Fig. 87. Now, lay the forepart right side up on the bench, and on it lay the facing right side down. Baste the facing onto the forepart, going down from the shoulder along the crease of the revers, continuing down the front 1 in. inside the edge. Remember to baste flat on the bench; it is impossible to baste such long areas while holding the work in the hand. Carry a second basting along the edge of the facing nearest the lining.

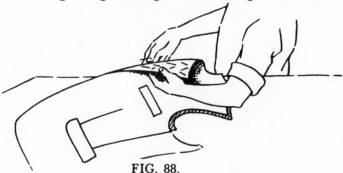

FIG. 88.

Fig. 88. Next, baste-on the part of the facing that is to cover the revers. Do this with a number of wide padding stitches while curling the revers with the left hand. This curling is very important in order that the revers will roll freely when the coat is completed.

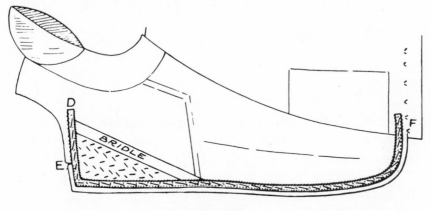

FIG. 89.

Fig. 89. You may now begin to baste the staytape around the edges of the fronts. Start (on the right forepart) at the top, D; baste with a padding stitch, laying the tape moderately tight so that the edge of the front is drawn in perceptibly. Let the tape pass only ⅛ in. beyond the edge of the canvas — just enough to take a seam without sewing through the canvas. When the tape is completely basted, hand-sew its inner edge to the canvas all around, making the stitches fine and close. Then press the tape flat with the iron, using very little moisture on the sponge. Finally, sew on the machine, along the tape's outer edge, from F, the point where the facing meets the lining at the bottom, up to E, the notch of the revers. On the left forepart, the seam is taken from top to bottom, E to F. Trim the edges all around to have them thin and straight when turned.

Fig. 90. Remove all bastings from the tape and facing, and turn the front right side out. Very carefully, baste along the front edge turning it flat and straight as it is to be in the finished

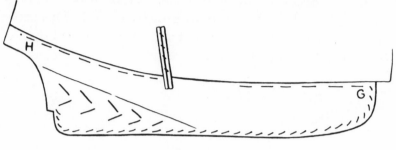

FIG. 90.

garment. Then baste the revers in a natural roll, using three or four rows of wide padding stitches. Finally, baste the facing to the coat along the lining, G to H.

Now, lift the lining out of the way in order to work inside the coat. Fasten the edge of the facing to the canvas, with a wide, loose hand-stitching from H to G, skipping the area of the breast pocket. Tack the canvases to the pockets at their front corners with a number of strong stitches.

After you have made up both fronts in this manner you may turn to the next operation which is basting-in the body lining, Fig. 91 to 93.

Basting-in the body lining

Fig. 91. Baste the linings of the foreparts in the manner illustrated, beginning 2 in. from the top, and about 2 in. inside the armhole, as at A; continuing down around the armhole to B, which is 2 in. inside the side seam; thence down to C, which is 2 in. from the bottom, and turning toward D. Treat the left side in the same manner. Baste the lining with some fullness in it, for a lining fitted too closely always gives trouble.

Fig. 92. Make chalk lines on the linings along the run of the coat side seams, as from E to F and G to H. Baste the back linings to the forepart linings, laying edges of backs along chalk lines. Then sew the seams E-F and G-H on the machine.

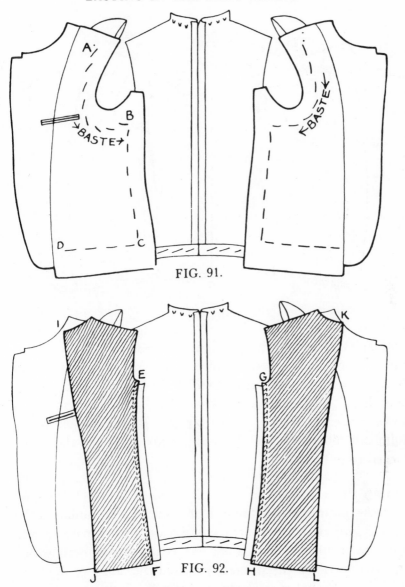

FIG. 91.

FIG. 92.

Now folding the coat wrong side out, pull the two half-backs together and take the center-back seam, joining I-J to K-L.

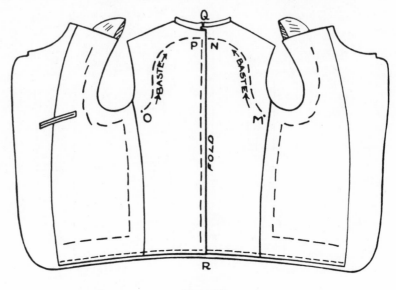

FIG. 93.

Fig. 93. Turn the lining right side out, and lay the coat flat on the bench, in the manner depicted. Baste the back lining from M to N and from O to P, allowing the excess width to gather at the center of the back. Baste this excess in a fold down the center of the back as from Q to R. Finally turn in the lining all along the bottom, basting about ½ in. above the turned edge.

Closing the shoulders

Now, baste together the coat shoulder seams, fulling-in the back shoulders on the front; sew the seams on the machine and press them open. Then, laying the coat shoulder wrong side out on the end of the sleeveboard, fold the lining of the back shoulder onto that of the front shoulder; baste it thus and stitch the seam by hand.

This completes the body section of the coat, and you may give your attention to the collar.

Cutting and basting on the collar foundation

Collars almost never give trouble if a little preliminary study of their construction is made.

Collars are composed of three layers: the *undercollar,* the *linen canvas,* and the *outside collar.* The undercollar is usually cut out of a piece of special undercollar cloth rather than from the cloth of the garment. This material is preferable to the cloth, because when sewn on the raw edge, as it must be around the neckline, it does not ravel as would regular suiting cloth. The collar canvas is also specially made for its purpose, being sized for permanent stiffness. The outside collar is a single piece of cloth cut on the fold of the goods, as shown in Fig. 28.

The undercollar and the canvas are both cut in two pieces and on the bias to permit stretching of their edges, Fig. 99. The halves are sewn together, and the canvas is attached to the undercollar with close rows of padding stitches. Thus joined, they form the foundation for the outside collar to be sewn on, Figs. 100, 101.

In tailoring parlance, a collar has two parts: a "stand", the portion which stands up from the shoulder seam; and the "fall", the portion folding down from the crease and covering up the "stand." To begin to understand collar construction, it is important to view the stand of the collar as the base collar of which the fall is merely the replica.

Collars are simple, the only considerations in their planning and cutting being the length of the crease edge and the angle of the gorge curve. The former is obtained by a simple measurement, Fig. 94; the latter by adjustment at the fitting, Fig. 104. The following exercise is recommended to teach the principles involved in the construction of collars.

Cut a strip of paper 1¼ in. wide (which is the width of the stand) and pin it onto the neck section of the coat, so that its upper edge runs in conjunction with the crease of the revers, and its lower edge sets just above the level of the nape of the neck, Fig. 94. Cut the strip at both sides, as at A, where the revers crease transverses the curve of the gorge. Now, merely

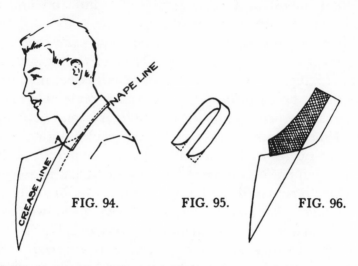

FIG. 94.   FIG. 95.   FIG. 96.

FIGS. 94, 95, 96. Illustrating the principles involved in the construction of collars. FIG. 94 — A strip of paper, 1¼ in. wide, is laid around the subject's neck, its upper edge continuous with the crease of the revers, its lower edge in line with the nape of the neck. The strip is then cut at both sides, as at A, where the revers crease transverses the curve of the gorge. FIG. 95 — The lower corners of the strip are rounded off, completing a proven pattern for the "stand" of the collar. FIG. 96 — The "fall" of the collar, shown by the shaded portion, has been "grown-on" to the stand.

by rounding off the lower end corners of this strip of paper, you obtain a reliable pattern of the stand of the collar, Fig. 95. The upper edge of this strip is the accurate crease length of the finished collar. And, by drawing a chalk line along its lower edge, on the coat, you determine exactly the location of the seam of the finished collar.

Remove this paper strip from the coat, fold it in half and lay it on the bias on the undercollar cloth, marking all around it and adding to it the "fall" section of the collar to the specifications given under Fig. 97. It is not necessary to plan the exact shape of the fall of the collar at this stage, the only care being that its width be generous and its ends of more than sufficient length, Fig. 96.

The formulas for cutting collars follow, Figs. 97 and 98.

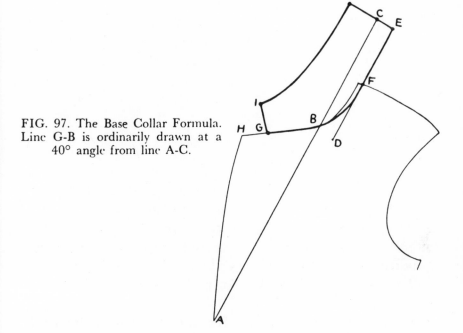

FIG. 97. The Base Collar Formula.
Line G-B is ordinarily drawn at a
40° angle from line A-C.

Fig. 97. *The base collar formula.* Suitable for all coats having a long revers, such as the two-button style and the double-breasted.

Place the forepart of the coat pattern on a piece of drafting paper, and extend the crease of the revers, A-B, up to C.

Line D-E is 1⅛ in. from B-C. (It may be made 1¼ in. for a higher collar.)

E from F is the width of upper back of the coat (1 to 10, Fig. 18).

G from H is 1½ in.

I from G is 1¾ in.

J from C is 1⅞ in. Curve very gently from I to J.

Line J-E is at right angles with line B-C.

Line I-G is at right angles with line H-B.

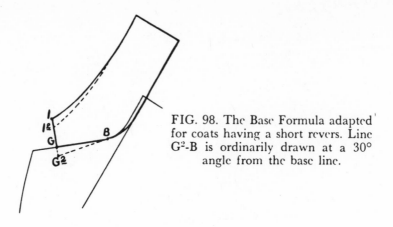

FIG. 98. The Base Formula adapted for coats having a short revers. Line G^2-B is ordinarily drawn at a 30° angle from the base line.

Fig. 98. *The base formula adapted for coats having a short revers,* such as the three-button, single-breasted style.

The pronounced rounding of the collar at B in Fig. 97 is not suitable for the three-button coat, for the reason that such rounding does not permit the revers to fall in the desired roll.

The less rounded type of collar needed is obtained by dropping the point G about ¾ in. to G^2, and also dropping the point I to I^2 the same amount. It will be found good practice to cut all collars in this manner, later trimming away the triangle G-G^2-B, if necessary.

CUTTING AND BASTING ON THE COLLAR FOUNDATION

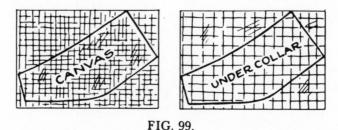

FIG. 99.

Fig. 99. Cut one collar out of collar canvas, and one out of undercollar cloth. Cut both on the bias, as shown; and, of course, on the double, to obtain two halves for each collar.

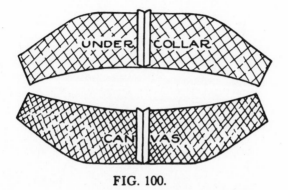

FIG. 100.

Fig. 100. Sew together the halves of the canvas and those of the undercollar, and press open the seam.

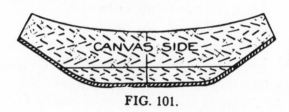

FIG. 101.

Fig. 101. Baste the canvas collar to the undercollar, the seams facing each other. Pad the canvas to the undercollar, all over, using a close stitch. Pare the canvas away ⅛ in. inside the bottom edge, and draw a chalk line 1⅛ in. from the bottom edge.

FIG. 102.

Fig. 102. Fold the collar on the line, canvas side out, and dry-press while slightly stretching the edges of the fall.

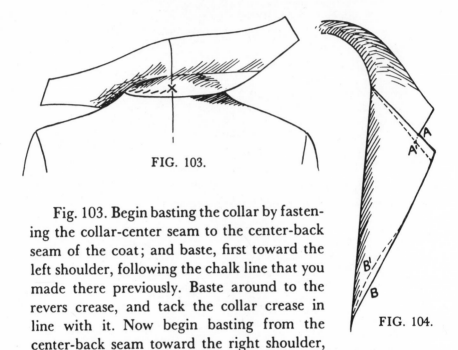

FIG. 103.

FIG. 104.

Fig. 103. Begin basting the collar by fastening the collar-center seam to the center-back seam of the coat; and baste, first toward the left shoulder, following the chalk line that you made there previously. Baste around to the revers crease, and tack the collar crease in line with it. Now begin basting from the center-back seam toward the right shoulder, doing the same thing. Baste the collar on fair, neither tight nor loose.

Fig. 104. Now place the coat on the form or dummy, and pin the ends of the collar to the top of the revers, at the angle in which they most properly command the roll of the revers. Remember that the revers are pressed flat only where they meet the collar, but should roll below that point, the roll being most pronounced at B. Note, however, that the roll at B is controlled by the angle of the revers at A. If point A is lowered to A^1 on the collar end, the roll of revers at B will increase, as at B^1; if point A is raised on the collar end, the revers no longer roll at B, but lie flat. The beginner should practice pinning the collar ends to the revers at various angles; and, when the adjustment seems correct, he may remove the coat from the form and complete the basting to the notch of the revers.

BASTING IN THE SLEEVES

From time immemorial sleeves have been the headache of tailors, and their setting still remains the most difficult task in coatmaking. It is entirely true that you can judge a tailor's ability by the sleeves he puts in, and that it is the workmanship in the shoulder region of the coat that makes or mars the entire garment.

There are very difficult problems about sleeves because so many factors defying analysis are involved in their relation to the armholes into which they are to sew. No two of them go in exactly the same way. However, the persevering student can master sleeves as he can other operations, for there are methods of cutting and putting in sleeves that are quite reliable.

As to cutting, I must forewarn the beginner of the difficulties incurred by the practice of cutting the sleeves at the same time as the body of the coat. As, at the try-on stage, the coat body may require radical changes in the armhole and shoulder section, the original calculations upon which the sleeves were drafted are upset, the notches may be thrown out of place, and the armholes made larger or smaller than originally planned. The armholes being altered, the sleeves also must be altered.

Fortunately, the alterations are not difficult, mainly involving changes in the height or the width of the sleeve hole. Directions for making such changes are given in Figs. 113-116.

Preparing the armholes

The first requisite for putting in good sleeves is the preparation of suitable armholes in the body of the coat. These should measure about one half the coat size, that is, half of the subject's chest measurement. Thus, a size 40 coat should measure about 20 in. around the armhole. Also both armholes should be of the same size, a requisite necessitating an alteration when one shoulder is over ½ in. lower than the other. In such a case, the tailor is obliged to take in the seam of the low shoulder to the extent of twice the amount that the shoulder is lower; and

101

to scoop the base of the armhole the amount that the shoulder is lower, Fig. 107. This alteration does make the coat lopsided, but it equalizes the sizes of the armholes. As for fit, there is no means of dealing with the lopsided subject, except to make his coat also lopsided.

ALTERING FOR LOW SHOULDER

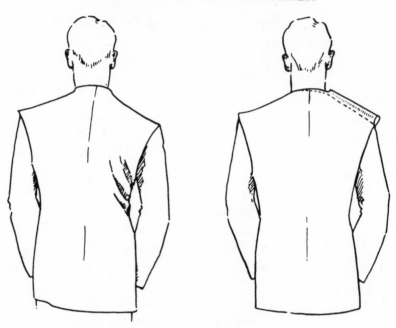

FIG. 105. Showing the right shoulder lower than the left, a very common defect. Note the unsightly wrinkles back of the right arm.

FIG. 106. Correcting the defect by pinning out the excess in a fold along the shoulder seam.

Padding a pronouncedly lower shoulder in the attempt to make it look as high as its companion will result in an elongated, oversized armhole that will require a similarly elongated, oversized sleevehole. However, when the shoulder is only $\frac{1}{2}$ in. lower than its companion, padding it is the proper thing to do, and no alteration is called for.

The alteration for a low shoulder is illustrated in Figs. 105-107.

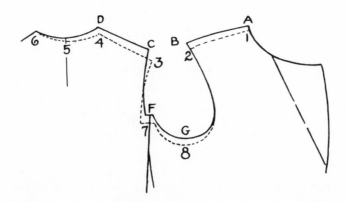

FIG. 107. Assuming that the shoulder is ¾ in. lower than its companion, the forepart at A-B must be lowered to line 1-2, and the backpart C-D lowered to line 3-4. The amount lowered below B and C is the full ¾ in.; below A and D, ⅜ in. F goes down ¾ in. to 7, and the base of the armhole at G is scooped ¾ in. down to 8. The back neck, 4-5-6, is relined on the skew as shown.

Staying the armholes

Having equalized the size of the armholes, the next step is to stay their edges.

At the try-on a chalk line was drawn indicating the run of the sleeve seam all around the armhole. Now, just outside this line, run a drawing-in stitch all around the hole to keep its edges from stretching along the upper half, and to draw-in the edges along the lower half. This stitch, which is done with a doubled, twisted length of strong basting cotton, gives an elastic quality to the armhole edge not obtainable with staytape. In execution, it is much like the buttonhole stitch, except that the needle is held pointing toward the left, the stitches being taken one behind the other toward the right. Figs. 108 to 111 demonstrate.

As already said, only the lower half of the armhole should be drawn in; the upper half should only be stayed to prevent stretching. The drawing-in gives to the lower half of the hole a "cup" shape which, while very desirable there, is not at all proper in the upper half. Fig. 112. After the armhole has been

THE DRAWING-IN STITCH

FIG. 108. The thread is knotted and run through at A, drawn and held at B with the right hand. Left hand holds edge·of material.

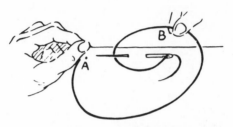

FIG. 109. Second movement. B has been drawn around the point of the needle, and the operator needs only to draw out the needle and pull the thread toward the right to complete the stitch.

FIG. 110. A completed stitch is shown magnified, and the needle has been inserted to begin another stitch.

FIG. 111. Several completed stitches. In actual size they are taken about ½ in. apart. Stitches are taken one behind the other toward the right.

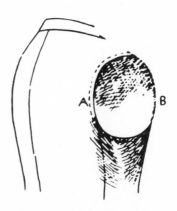

FIG. 112. The well-prepared armhole is cup shaped in the lower half, as below A and B, being drawn in noticeably in that section by the stitch.

stayed all around, its edge should be dry-pressed in order to flatten any little ridges caused by the drawing-in. When this is done, the armhole measures about ⅝ in. less than it did before the staying was done.

Preparing the sleeves

The sleeve topsides are to be slightly stretched at the hollow of the inseam, L, Fig. 21; then sewn to the undersides, great care being taken to seam them without any suggestion of twisting. The seams are then pressed open. The sleeveholes in men's coats, if properly drafted, should now measure 2¾ in. more in circumference than the armholes of the coat. Of this 2¾ in., 2 in. is to be distributed around the upper part of the armhole, from front notch to back notch. The remaining ¾ in. is distributed along the bottom and back section of the hole where little fullness is needed. The sleevehole of a woman's coat should measure about 2 or 2¼ in. more than the armhole in which it is to go, of which 1½ to 1¾ in. will be distributed around the upper section of the hole.

As regards fullness, it must be remembered that cloths vary in the amount that can be put in. In hard cloths, like gabardine for example, excess fullness cannot be pressed in without forming a pinched seam. When working in such cloths it is wise to cut the sleeve on the smaller side, so that the usual 2¾ in. of fullness will be reduced by ½ in. In soft goods, like tweeds, where much fullness can be pressed in, 3 in. or 3¼ in. of fullness can be put in. In all cases, it is good practice to put in as much fullness around the crown of the sleeve as can be pressed in without forming a pinched seam.

ALTERING THE SLEEVE

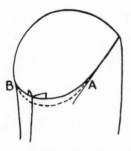

FIG. 113. Adding height to the sleevehole by scooping it around the bottom. Scoop from A to B — not beyond either point.

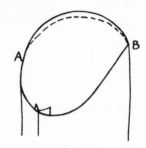

FIG. 114. Decreasing height of sleevehole by trimming around the crown.

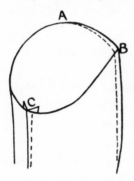

FIG. 115. Decreasing the sleeve width. Trim from A to B, gradually widening toward B, and continue trimming down to the elbow. This is done to the topside of sleeve only; underside is narrowed at C.

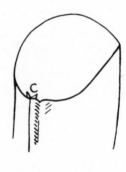

FIG. 116. Widening the sleeve by letting out the underside at C.

The height of the sleevehole should measure the same, or a bit over, that of the armhole. If the sleevehole is too short vertically, it will have to be scooped at the bottom, Fig. 113. If

106

it is too long vertically, it will have to be trimmed along the top, Fig. 114. If it is too wide, material must be removed at the back seam, Fig. 115. If too narrow, added width can be provided by letting out the inseam inlay, Fig. 116.

The diagonal of the underside of the sleeve should always be built on a triangle whose vertical side is 3½ in., and whose base is 3 in. Experience has shown that an underside so proportioned results in a well-draping back to the finished sleeve.

Basting-in

In custom work, the balance notches in the sleeve and armhole are not regarded as reliable guides, but merely as approximations. The tailor prefers to guide the pitch of the sleeves by the chalk mark he has made at the try-on, in line with the front of the subject's wrist. Some persons carry their arms backward, others forward; and for this reason, following the notches slavishly is not good practice, even though normally, doing so results in a satisfactory hang of the sleeve.

Always baste in the *left* sleeve first; it always goes in more naturally because the basting can be started from the front notch, as it can not on the right sleeve. Turn the coat inside out and tack the front notch of the sleeve to the front notch of the armhole; tack also the back seam of the sleeve to the back notch of the armhole. Start at the front notch, basting *on* the sleeve, and carefully distributing the fullness as you go. Carry the basting toward the top, around the crown to the back notch, then down the back toward the underarm. Remember that most of the fullness goes in the upper half of the armhole, and that what little of it goes in the lower half is mostly confined to the back, just below the notch. There is hardly any fullness introduced along the base of the armhole.

Now, examine the hang of your sleeve by putting your fist in the shoulder of the coat and holding it up in its natural drape; or place the coat on the form; or try it on yourself. The front edge of the sleeve bottom should fall about 1½ in. in front of the chalk mark at the wrist, and the sleeve should fall perfectly straight without any breaks or fluting. (If you are trying the coat on yourself, you must naturally hold your wrist where your client does.) If the sleeve breaks into several folds along the back seam, it is pitched too far toward the front; you must lower the front notch of the sleeve about 1/4 in. below the front notch of the armhole, and lift the sleeve backseam 1/4 in. above the back notch of the armhole. If the sleeve breaks along the front, it is pitched too far toward the back; you will have to raise the front notch of the sleeve about 1/4 in. above the front notch of the armhole, and to lower the sleeve backseam 1/4 in. below the back notch of the armhole. When analyzed, these alterations prove to be mere rotations of the sleevehole either frontward or backward. Of course the rotating action must not be overdone, for even such a small quantity as 1/4 in. can throw the sleeve bottom definitely backward or forward.

Occasionally, in dealing with subjects of abnormal posture, you will mistrust the guidance of the notches, and want to determine the sleeve pitch by the wrist position only. To do this, place the coat on the form or dummy, and hang the sleeve in its position in the armhole by a single pin at the top, balancing it by one pin each side. By this simple means, you can often make the sleeve accord with the wrist position with very little effort.

Basting in the sleeves is a matter learned only by doing. One must be willing to baste, rip, and rebaste, until the desired pitch and drape are obtained. It often takes a long time to do this, especially for the beginner who is working on a pattern of his own construction — that is, an untested pattern. During my apprenticeship, I once or twice spent half a day basting in some stubborn sleeves. It was time well spent, which taught me lessons I should never have learned had I just hurried along. Sleeves often make us sweat and sigh, but with determination we can win the victory over them as with any other part of the coat.

A properly cut and set sleeve should fall straight, without diagonal folds or breaks in the line of the front or of the back.

The student should notice the hang of sleeves on coats put out by the better manufacturers, whose garments are cut on painstakingly designed patterns, and show the sleeve at its best. There is a beautiful, characteristic front roll, a smooth, rounded crown, and a characteristic drape of the back which should be independently studied, for it is very different from that of the front.

Having basted in the left sleeve, no trouble is usually had with the right one. Merely measure the distance from the seam of the left shoulder, down to the back seam of the left sleeve; then measure the same amount from the seam of right shoulder, down toward the back, and make a chalk line. This is the point where you will tack the back seam of your right sleeve. Measure, again, on the left sleeve, the distance from its inseam to the underarm seam in the coat; then measure, on the right sleeve, the same distance from the underarm seam, and make a chalk mark where the right sleeve inseam will be tacked. Using these guide marks will insure basting the right sleeve in exactly the same way that you have the left one.

THE SECOND TRY-ON

The coat, at this stage, is ready for the second try-on. The sleeves having been basted in without linings, the tailor can change them anywhere without hindrance. The collar being only built in foundation, it may easily be displaced and re-basted. The fronts being unstitched, and not cut for button-holes, they may be altered by ripping open the facing.

This try-on is for the following three main purposes:

(1) To see if the sleeveheads look well, and that the sleeves drop down straight, without breaks or flutings, at the proper pitch; also to determine their length precisely.

(2) To see if the collar sits rightly, is of the proper length, and commands the revers nicely.

(3) To see if the lap of the front is even, or if the fronts need to be altered in some way before stitching the edges and cutting the buttonholes.

109

In general, follow the fitting procedure outlined for the first try-on, rechecking on the length and size of the coat, the fit of the shoulders, and the other features mentioned in the chapter on fitting.

If many changes have to be made, plan for a third try-on. Do not work blindly for fear of inconveniencing your client with repeated try-ons. Have four try-ons if necessary; only make the coat right, and you will be liked for it in the end.

PUTTING ON THE OUTSIDE COLLAR

The outside collar can be sewn onto the collar foundation by hand or on the sewing machine. As the hand method is long and difficult for beginners, the more rapid and equally satisfactory machine method is demonstrated in Figs. 117 to 125. A collar so finished has a straight neat edge which, when closely trimmed from the inside, looks quite as thin as one sewn by hand.

FINISHING THE COLLAR

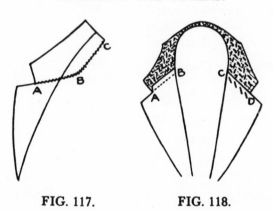

FIG. 117.   FIG. 118.

Fig. 117. Fell the bottom edge of the undercollar all around the neck, sewing by hand on the raw edge. On the left side (shown), fell from C to B to A. On the right side, fell from the end of the collar, working toward the center back.

Fig. 118. Chalk-mark a diagonal line along the top edge of each revers, as at A-B. Turn in and baste the revers edge on the line, as from C to D. Hand-sew the turned-in edge to the canvas, with invisible, loose and rather wide stitches, as from C to D.

Fig. 119. This figure shows the coat turned inside out. Continue turning in the revers edge about 1 in. inside the coat. At E, nick the facing, and hand-sew the facing and lining on their raw edge clear around the neck.

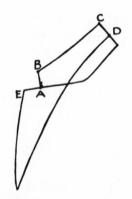

Fig. 120. Now, with a freshly sharpened piece of chalk, design on the undercollar the outline of the finished collar. B from A is 1⅝ in. and C from D is 1⅞ in.; and only slightly curve the line from B to C. A inside E is 1½ in. Line A-B is at right angles with E-A. Trim the undercollar on these chalk lines, and then trim the canvas ¼ in. inside the undercollar edge all around.

Fig. 121. Now take the outside collar, and stretch the edges of both the fall and the stand, using very little moisture. Confine the stretching to about 4 in. each side of the collar center; do not stretch the corners.

FIG. 122.

Fig. 122. Baste the outside collar onto and facing the undercollar, as shown. First, baste it flat along the crease; then baste all around the edges, fulling it a bit at the corners as from A to B and B to C.

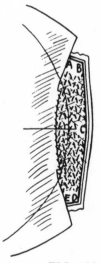

Fig. 123. Lay the collar, canvas side up, on the sewing machine and sew around it, from A to B, C, D, and E, seaming along the edge of the canvas but not through it. Then trim the outside collar all around, and especially close at the corners.

FIG. 123.   FIG. 124.

Fig. 124. Turn the outside collar right side out, basting the edges all around in a finished manner. Then baste it along the crease of the collar, smoothing it flat as you go.

Fig. 125. Turn in and baste the bottom edges of the outside collar flush with the top edges of the revers. Join these two

FIG. 125.

edges by hand-felling with a very close invisible stitch. Of course, the section of the collar inside the coat need not be stitched with as much care. A "hanger," made from a bit of lining, should be inserted at center back.

FINISHING THE SLEEVES

Steps in finishing the sleeveheads (not illustrated)

(1) After the sleeves have been basted in satisfactorily, they may be sewn on the machine, using a close stitch. Seam with the sleeve edge topmost, and be careful to go in a straight line, as any small crook will show when the seam is pressed open.

(2) Pull out the bastings from the seams, lay the inverted sleevehead on the sleeveboard, and press the seam open around the top, from front notch to back notch.

(3) Turn the coat right side out, place the fist in the shoulder, and run a basting around the armhole just inside the seam. Baste with a through-stitch, passing the needle back and forth through all layers (cloth, padding and lining) and smoothing the lining in place from the inside as you go.

(4) Turning the coat inside out again, stitch through all layers, fastening the cloth, canvas, padding, and lining to the seam of the sleeve, all around. Use a strong, doubled thread of basting cotton, but have the stitches very loose in the upper half of the armhole. This done, you may remove the basting previously done from the outside of the coat shoulder.

(5) Trim the excess canvas, lining, and padding all around the hole. Trim quite close along the lower half of the hole; but, along the upper half, allow an extra $1/4$ in. of canvas and padding to project beyond the edge of the seam.

113

(6) Cut two strips of cotton felt, about 4 by 11 in.; fold each lengthwise; and fold a second time. Run a machine seam through the thickest part, using a widened stitch. Sew one of those strips in the upper half of each sleeve, laying the strip on top of the projecting canvas, and having it extend from the front notch to 2 in. below the back notch. Sew these strips with a close but rather loose stitch. Their function is to give the sleeve crown a smooth, rounded appearance.

NOTE: The instructions that precede will best be understood if the student will rip the sleeve of an old but well-constructed coat. Rip the lining, and note how the strip of wadding is fastened in the seam; how all the layers are stitched to the seam; how the seam is pressed open and trimmed.

FINISHING THE SLEEVE BOTTOMS

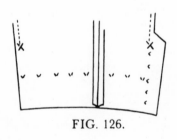

FIG. 126.

Fig. 126. The sleeve is here represented open and flat, to demonstrate more clearly the method of making the vent. Sewn up, the two seam ends marked X are coincident.

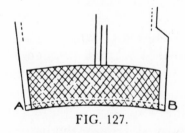

FIG. 127.

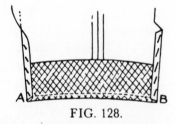

FIG. 128.

Fig. 127. Cut two strips of wigan on the bias, the length of the sleeve bottom and about 3 in. wide. Machine-sew one of these along the bottom of each sleeve, as from A to B. Trim the wigan ¼ in. inside both ends, as shown.

Fig. 128. Turn in and baste the ends at A and B.

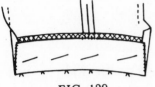

FIG. 129.

Fig. 129. Turn up bottoms in the threadmarks, basting them neatly. Fell the turned-up ends with a fine stitch.

FIG. 130.

Fig. 130. Sleeve is shown turned inside out. Stitching of the underlap of the vent is done by hand, in rectangular pattern, as from B to C to D to B. The stitching must be invisible from the outside of the sleeve. The turn-up is tacked to the seam only at E.

FIG. 131.

Fig. 131. Sleeve turned right side out and completed. Lowest button is $1\frac{1}{2}$ in. from the bottom. Button centers are $\frac{5}{8}$ in. apart, and $\frac{5}{8}$ in. from the back seam.

Putting in the sleeve linings

The sleeve linings are cut on the pattern of the sleeve itself, and the two parts sewn together as were the sleeves. To baste them in, turn the coat sleeves inside out, laying out the underside of lining (also wrong side out), face to face with the underside of the sleeve, the lining being placed high enough to allow for a $\frac{1}{2}$ in. turn-in around the top.

Fasten the inseam of the lining flat onto the inseam of the sleeve with wide, loose stitches. Do the same along the back seam. This secures the lining to both sleeve seams, preparatory to the felling around the top and bottom.

To fell the top properly, the beginner may have to resort to basting, but the experienced operator merely tacks the lining seams to the sleeve seams and turns in the lining as he goes along. Strong silk is used and the stitches are placed closely and made fine.

Felling the linings at the bottom is simple and requires no instruction.

FINISHING THE FRONTS

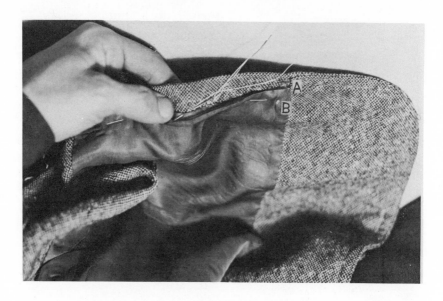

FIG. 132. Felling the lining along the coat bottom. The bottom of the coat is shown hemmed, the seam of the facing hand-stitched at A, and the lining basted from B. Note how the tailor lifts the fold of the lining in order to sew it with a pleat. Linings must always be sewn with such a pleat of reserve material at the bottom.

Felling the bottom

The hem of the bottom is sewn by hand with widely spaced "blind" stitches, i.e., stitches that do not quite penetrate the cloth and are invisible from the outside of the garment. Then, the facing is stitched finely along its inner corner at the bottom, Fig. 132, A. Next, the lining itself is turned in about ¼ in. from the coat bottom, and basted ½ in. above its turned edge, Fig. 132, B. The lining is then sewn to the coat bottom in line with this basting, by lifting up the edge with the point of the needle and sewing the lower layer only to the coat. The pleat so formed acts as a reservoir of material should the lining shrink or prove short after pressing.

Stitching the front edges

The stitching of the edges on the machine is done in three lays. Each front from the topmost button down to the round of the bottom is stitched from the outside of the coat, i.e., with the coat lying right side up on the sewing machine. Thread ends are left long at the beginning and end of the seams to permit their being drawn in between the layers of cloth. The revers and collar section of the coat are sewn in one continuous seam, from the topmost button of the right side to the top buttonhole of the left, the revers and collar also being sewn from the outside of the coat. Here, too, the ends of the thread are left about 4 in. long to facilitate their being drawn into the cloth. It is slovenly practice to tie knots in the thread ends, or to run the stitching back and forth on the fronts of the coat. One should put the thread ends two together through the eye of the needle and draw them into the cloth without knotting.

The seam of the edge is usually taken a small ⅛ in. wide, and is kept even by using a small gage on the foot of the machine. In sports coats, the seam may be made ¼ in. from the edge.

Buttonholes

The buttonholes on the front of the coat are cut 4 in. apart and with their eyes ⅝ in. inside the edge. The one in the revers (which may be omitted in a woman's coat) is 1¾ in. down from top of revers and ¾ in. inside its front edge, and is cut without an eye.

For complete instructions on cutting and making the buttonholes, see the chapter on hand-sewing.

Pressing

The buttonholes being made, remove all the bastings out of the coat (except the thread marking the lap of the fronts) and prepare to devote *at least* 1½ hours to the job of pressing it. This is the minimum time required to press a new coat — a fact that novices might well recall when attempting to do the job in half an hour.

First, dry-press all the edges from their reverse sides; for the beauty of the finished garment depends to a large extent on its thin, flat edges. Dry-pressing of edges is done not with the usual, wet press cloth but with a piece of drilling about 18 in. long, whose surface is dampened with the sponge before each lay. Pressing in this way necessarily results in glossy areas, but this does not matter. For the present, aim primarily at flattening or "setting" the garment; a bit of steam will remove the gloss, later. Keep the iron at medium heat, and do not leave it too long in any one place, for it is easy to scorch the cloth when dry-pressing.

All edges are pressed a little more than the width of the iron all around. The revers and collars are pressed from their backs, but the fronts below the revers are pressed from the inside (facing side) of the coat.

This done, lay the coat on the sleeveboard around which you are to rotate it while pressing. You will now use the press cloth, but will wring out the water especially strenuously.

Begin with the left front, so that the pressed part will fall frontward on the bench, where it will be out of your way. Use the beater freely as you work, especially on the mouths of pockets and the seams that prove obstinate.

Three lays are usually required on each front, and three on the back — nine lays in all, in a coat of average size. The flap on the pocket, after being pressed, is lifted up, and its outline on the coat front is pressed out.

Once the body of the coat is done, turn to the shoulders and collar. The shoulders are pressed on the end of the sleeveboard, as is also the collar, after which the latter is creased all around

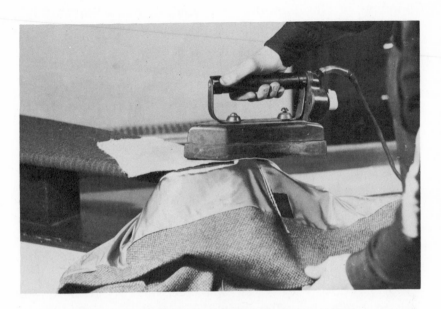

FIG. 133. Creasing the lower half of the armhole.

to the top of each revers. Finally, press the surfaces of the revers on the edge of the sleeveboard, using the beater to make them lie as smoothly as possible, but being careful to preserve the soft roll as depicted in Fig. 104.

You may now turn to the most difficult part of coat pressing, the sleeveheads and the sleeves. Press the sleeves while laying the body of the coat in front (or in back) of the sleeveboard to avoid wrinkling it. The sleeves are pressed lengthwise in two lays. The sleevehead, however, is pressed while holding the coat shoulder on the fist, placing a small pad between fist and area pressed. To crease the sleeve, turn the coat inside out, placing the end of the sleeveboard in the armhole so that the "armpit" area of the coat body is uppermost. Press all around the lower half of the armhole in this way, creasing it in the seam against the body of the coat. This operation is illustrated in Fig. 133.

This first pressing, as has been said, is done rather dry, ignoring the shininess that appears in spots. The coat is then hung up, or placed on the form, and allowed to set overnight. The next day, it is taken up again, lightly steamed with a damp cloth to remove the shine, and touched up in any part that seems faulty.

I advocate that the student deliberately press his coat in two sessions rather than to try to do it all at one time. In this way, he will save himself much nerve exhaustion and do a better job.

Rayon linings, such as are commonly used in coats nowadays, require a rather cool iron, as they readily burn to a crisp when too much heat touches them. If there are deep creases in the lining, the tailor dampens them with the moist sponge and applies the iron directly. As a rule, one presses linings by applying the iron directly to them, without intervening press cloth.

In garments with velvet collars, one must always be careful not to touch the collar with the iron. Velvet can only be steamed through; the steam being applied from the back of the collar. Lay the flatiron on its back, between props, and spread on it the doubled press cloth; then lay the back of the collar in contact with the cloth. As the steam rises through the velvet, lightly brush it with the whisk broom until it lies flat and is of even sheen.

Do not apply the iron directly to the silk facings of a tuxedo or full-dress coat. Press from the back of the revers.

Sewing on the buttons

Buttons are sewn on a coat only after it has been pressed.

To locate the position of those to go on the front, turn the coat inside out, laying the fronts one on the other, with the front edges and the bottoms even. The front with the buttonholes in it (left one in a man's coat; right one in a woman's) should be uppermost.

Scrape some chalk through the eye of each buttonhole, thus making a mark for each button center on the button side of the coat.

The button centers should be measured ⅝ in. inside the threadmarks placed along the lap of the coat before pressing.

On the sleeve bottoms, the three button centers should be marked ⅝ in. apart, the lowest one being 1½ in. from the bottom edge. They should be ⅝ in. from the back seam.

The buttons of the front must be sewn with a "neck." Sew them loosely, therefore, lifting them ⅛ in. above the cloth as you stitch. Four through stitches — two through each set of holes — of stout, double-twisted thread are sufficient. Then wind thread around the stitching, between the button and the cloth, to form the neck.

SEQUENCE OF OPERATIONS IN MAKING A COAT

1. Drafting the pattern.
2. Making the canvas interlinings.
3. Cutting the coat, and threadmarking the parts.
4. Basting up for the try-on (body part only).
5. The first try-on.
   (a) Sewing the darts.
   (b) Basting in the canvases.
   (c) Basting the foreparts to the backparts.
   (d) Putting in the shoulder pads.
6. Ripping apart, altering, and trimming the fronts.
7. Correcting the pattern.
8. Making the side pockets.
9. Making the outside breast pocket.
10. Cutting the linings, and making the inside breast pocket.
11. Making the fronts.
    (a) Rebasting in the canvases.
    (b) Padding the revers.
    (c) Trimming the canvases.
    (d) Staying, seaming and turning the edges.
12. Basting in the body lining.
13. Cutting and basting on the collar foundation.
14. Basting in the sleeves.
15. The second try-on.

16. Putting on the outside collar.
17. Finishing the sleeves.
18. Finishing the fronts.
19. Pressing.
20. Sewing on the buttons.

Chapter VIII

Trouser Making

MEASUREMENTS FOR A TROUSER

A TROUSER is composed of four panels of cloth, two to each leg, and the student should rip apart a pair of old ones in order to understand how these panels are joined together and shaped.

In the first edition of this work, it was advocated that all students learn to make their first trousers with the buttoned fly. This was not only because trousers had traditionally been made this way, but also because the legs could be completed separately before joining them; this also simplified the task of exposition.

However, since the slide fastener, or zipper, has come into universal use over the years, the author has perforce dropped all text and illustrations relating to the button fly in favor of construction with a zipper. In the future, zippers may be discarded for some other type of closure deemed more desirable, but for the present we must honor today's preferences.

The method advocated here has, in this writer's teaching experience, proved the most practical to the learner. It must be said, however, that the use of the zipper does make trouser construction a more complex job than was the case when buttons were used.

Only four main measurements are required in the drafting of trousers. These are: (1) the *inseam,* which is the inside seam of the leg measured from crotch to bottom, (2) the *outseam,* which is the over-all length of the trouser from the top of the waistband down to the bottom, measured along the outside seam, (3) the *waist,* and (4) the *seat.* Other auxiliary measurements that should be taken are the width of bottom, width of knee, and width of thigh, but these measurements are very nearly the same in the general run of trousers.

Unlike a coat, a trouser requires very little fitting if the measurements to which it was drafted and cut were taken accurately. It is a remarkably simple garment to plan and make, and many tailors finish their trousers without even a try-on.

In measuring, it is especially important to take the inseam and the outseam with absolute accuracy, as the difference between these two measurements determines how high the trousers will rise up the waist. For example, if the inseam is 30 in. and the outseam 41½ in., the "rise" will be 11½ in. — this being the distance from crotch to top edge of the trousers.

The most convenient way to get accurate inseam and outseam measurements, of course, is by measuring the trousers the subject has been wearing, if these are satisfactory. But when it becomes necessary to measure on the subject, follow these instructions carefully:

Have the subject stand with feet about 8 in. apart, with his trousers adjusted on his waist at the exact height he prefers to wear them. This gives you the proper starting point at the waist from which to take your outseam measurement. Place the end of the tape measure exactly on the top edge of the trouser, at the side seam, and measure clear down to the floor, deducting 1½ in. Measuring down to below the ankle, as is usually done by beginners, will not do, as the ankle is an indefinite zone. Measure always down to the floor and deduct whatever distance the trousers are to be worn from the floor (in most cases, 1½ in.)

Now, to obtain the correct inseam, have the client draw up

the trousers he is wearing to the point he deems them to feel most satisfactory in the crotch and seat regions. Then measure along the inseam from the crotch down to the floor, deducting 1½ in.

You now have measurements taken from one definite point to another definite point, not merely from one zone to another zone. You can rely on these measurements.

No precise rule can be given to determine the rise of trousers on the basis of a subject's height. One man of 5 ft. 10 in. in height may want a short rise of 11 in.—especially if he wears his trousers with a belt. Another man of the same height who is longer bodied, or who wears suspenders habitually, may want a rise of 12½ in. The rise of trousers runs from 11 in. to 14 in., 12½ in. being the average.

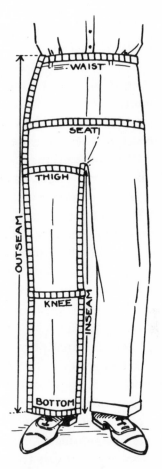

FIG. 134. Measuring for a trouser.

The waist measurement for the trouser offers no difficulty. It should be taken fair, neither tight nor loose, unless the subject has a preference either way.

The seat measurement, however, must be taken with a good deal of care, as trousers are drafted on proportions of this measurement (just as coats are drafted on proportions of the chest). It is not easy to take the seat accurately, as subjects are measured over their trousers, the folds and contents of which add considerably to the measurement. It is true that this meas-

125

urement must be taken very loosely if the trousers are to be sufficiently roomy for comfort, but there must be accuracy even in degree of looseness. Some tailors slacken the tape measure when taking this measurement, but I think the more accurate practice is to take it snug, and add 2 in. to it. This method has brought me uniformly accurate results, and gives a pant seat that is neither too close-fitting nor too roomy.

The measurement of the bottom of the trouser is 20 in. around for a man of average size, 19 in. for a small man, and 21 in. for a large man. The knee measurement for the average is 22 in.; for the small, 21; for the large, 23. The thigh measurement is useful only as a means of approximating the amount of material that must be added laterally in the crotch. Here people differ, some being full in the buttocks, wider laterally than the average; therefore, the crotch point of the backpart of the trouser must be extended beyond the quantity specified in the formula.

Do not attempt to measure the thigh of the trouser while it is being worn; but measure it while it is lying flat on the table, directly across the crotch.

Alterations are not usually difficult in trousers, but there is one point on which a little observation of your client will save you trouble. This has to do with posture. For while male subjects rarely give trouble due to wide hips or other peculiarities of form in the hip region, they do not all stand normally. Two types that necessitate changes in the pattern are frequently met with: (1) those that carry their hips pronouncedly forward, a posture that throws much looseness in the seat region, causing folds to appear beneath the buttocks. Such men usually have a habit of drawing their trousers high in front, as if sensing the actual shortness of the front in relation to the back. (2) Those that carry their hips and buttocks backward, a posture that causes the pants to strain over the buttocks and in the crotch, and to gather in small folds at the front. Directions for diagnosing these two posture problems and for altering the pattern in each case are given in Figs. 168-171.

THE TROUSER FORMULA

Outseam, 43 in.   Waist, 34 in.
Inseam, 31 in.   Bottom, 20 in.
Seat, 40 in. snug, plus 2 in. ease = 42 in.
Seat scale, 21 in.

The Forepart

2 from 1 is the outseam (43 in.).

3 from 1 is the inseam (31 in.).

4 from 1 is half the inseam plus 2 in. (17½ in.).

Square out from 1, 2, 3, and 4.

5 from 3 ⎫
6 from 1 ⎬ are ⅓ scale (7 in.). Rule line 6-5-A.

7 from 5 is ⅓ scale (7 in.).

8 is midway between 7 and 5. Square up from 8, to B.

9 above 8 is same distance as 7 from 8. Square across to 10.

11 from 2 is 1½ in. Drop vertically from 11 for 2 in. and curve into 10 as suggested.

Rule from B down to a point ¼ in. outside 9. Run a shallow curve into 7.

12, the fly notch, is 2 in. from 7.

13 from 6 ⎫
14 from 6 ⎬ are ¼ the bottom (5 in.).

Rule a straight line from 10 to 13, and from 7 to 14.

15 is ½ in. inside the straight line, and rule 10-15-13.

16 is ½ in. inside the straight line, and rule 7-16-14.

The top notch of the pocket, D, is 2¾ in. below 11.

The lower notch, E, is 6¼ in. from D.

The dashed line at the top is 1⅜ in. below the top line.

For all normal-waisted figures, a small pleat is advantageously sewn out at 17. This pleat which is located midway between A and 11, suppresses the waist a total of ⅜ in. in the half-pattern, and is sewn down about 2 in. below the dashed line. Its function is to introduce ease across the trouser front while shortening the belt. For large-waisted subjects, it is best to omit this pleat, leaving the forepart its full width.

The vertical dashed line runs 2¼ in. inside the front edge, B-12-7, and indicates the shape in which to cut the fly pieces.

Cut out the pattern of the forepart, notching it at 12, 3, 15, 16, D and E.

The Backpart

Lay the trouser forepart just cut on another length of pattern paper, weighing it down with stones or metal weights. Extend all horizontal lines of the forepart onto the new sheet: line 7-3 to 20 and 21, line B-11 to 22, line 15-16 to 19, and line 13-14 to 18.

$\left.\begin{array}{l}\text{18 from 14} \\ \text{19 from 16}\end{array}\right\}$ are 1 in.

20 from 7 is 2¼ in., and ¼ in. below the line.

21 from 3 is ¾ in.

Rule from 15 through 21, up to 22.

Square by line 21-22, to 23.

F is midway between A and B.

Rule from 9 through F, to 23.

Curve down from 9, running the line ¼ in. above the fly notch, and into 20. Curve the back line, 9-23, inwardly by ¼ in.

Point 24 is 4¾ in. both from the top and from the side of the backpart.

25 and 26 are each 2¾ in. from 24, and indicate the mouth of the pocket.

The dart, rising from 24, is cut ¾ in. wide at the mouth. Sewn, it will suppress the backpart 1¼ in.

The dashed line is 1⅜ in. below the top line, 22-23. Cut or fold both the forepart and the backpart on this dashed line. The removal of this 1⅜ in. leaves a generous ⅜ in. seam for seaming on the belt.

20 from 19 should be exactly the same length as 7 from 16.

If, after the dart is sewn, the backpart is still too wide across the top, narrow the pattern ½ in. or so inside 23.

Balance notches should be cut at 21, 15, and 19.

This trouser formula, besides being simple, is highly logical because it is constructed on the center line principle, and the legs may be widened or narrowed each side without impair-

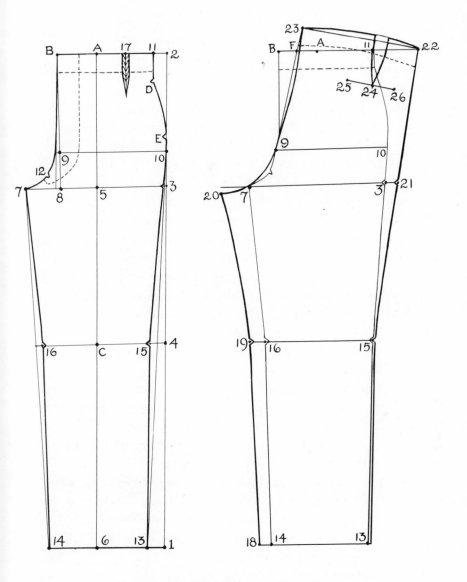

FIG. 135. The Trouser Formula.

ment of balance. Theoretically, the forepart is proportioned one quarter of the waist measure across the top, one quarter of the seat measure across the lower front, half of the knee measure across the knee region, and half the bottom measure across the bottom. Seam allowances are provided in the backpart. The formula produces a roomy garment across the front, with a clean fitting seat and straight hanging legs.

The thigh and knee measurements do not enter into the formula, which is self-adjusting in those regions. Occasionally, however, it is necessary to add width to the backpart outside point 20, and in such cases the thigh measure tells us approximately how much is needed there.

For a pleated trouser, split the pattern of the forepart down the center line, A-6, and paste between the two parts a wedge of pattern paper, opening the leg gradually from nothing at the bottom, to 2 in. at the top. The pleat, which will be 1 in. deep when sewn, may be turned either inwardly toward the fly, or outwardly toward the side. It should be pressed only after the legs have been pressed in the usual way. It may be noted that while pleats are comfortable, and pleasing in appearance on slender subjects, they do not look well on short or obese ones.

A finished trouser should measure about 3 in. more around the seat than the seat measurement taken snug. To measure the seat, spread the trouser, front side up, on the bench, measuring from one side to the other, and doubling the quantity. The waist can be measured in the same way.

Trousers always fit and look better around the waist when they are constructed with a belt, or waistband, — which is the reason why I have here presented a formula with this feature. The student is urged to get into the habit of making all his trousers this way, from the start.

In drafting trouser patterns, most of the old tailors altered the fly section for "dress provision," so-called. This meant increasing the width of one forepart (normally the left) at the

130

base curve of the fly, while decreasing the width of the other (right) forepart; the aim being to deflect the fly seam slightly toward the right, providing accommodation for the male organs on the left side. It will be noted that the trouser formula here ignores dress provision, which is a style feature of those times when snug trousers are fashionable.

In measuring for a trouser, note the shape of the pelvic region of your subject, especially when his seat measurement is unusually large. Some men are wide-hipped, but have ordinary buttocks; their trouser waist needs to be suppressed mainly in the side seams at the waist level. Others are narrow hipped but have rounded buttocks that jut out prominently, and their trouser waist needs to be suppressed by a widened dart in each backpart, or by introducing two darts there. For corpulent figures, or those with large waists, the dart is made very shallow, nothing being cut out from it; the suppression involves not much more than the two ¼-in. seams.

Cutting a trouser

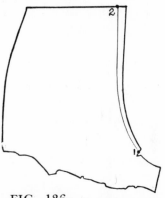

FIG. 136.

The forepart is cut with its side running along the edge of the cloth, as shown in Fig. 137, and a 5 in. addition is made at the bottom to provide material to make a cuff. This cuff addition should widen just a little, and not follow the taper of the leg.

In order that the fly may lap over the zipper, the right forepart of the trouser should be cut a bit wider than the left, as shown in Fig. 136. Line 1-2 here is the original front outline of the pattern. When tracing the pattern on the cloth, preparatory to cutting, add ¼ in. of width outside 1, gradually running up to ½ in. outside point 2.

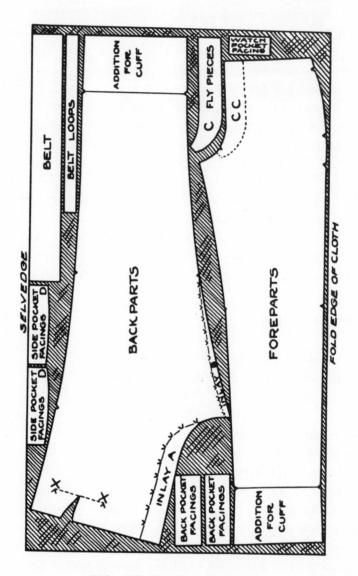

FIG. 137. Cutting a Trouser.

Trousers are cut with inlays only along the seat and thigh of the backparts, as shown. The inlay, A, is made about $1\frac{1}{2}$ in. wide at the top, tapering gradually as it goes down. The inlay, B, is about 1 in. wide and tapers down to the knee. (Some tailors have it go clear down to the bottom of the trousers.)

The belt is to be cut $2\frac{1}{2}$ in. wide; $1\frac{3}{4}$ being the width of the finished belt, plus $\frac{1}{4}$ in. for a seam, and $\frac{1}{2}$ in. to turn down at the top. It is to be cut 4 in. longer than half of the trouser waist. The belt-loop strips are cut $1\frac{1}{4}$ in. wide and 10 in. long, each strip to furnish four loops.

The fly pieces, C, are cut on the pattern of the forepart, C-C, and are made $2\frac{1}{4}$ in. wide, and $2\frac{1}{4}$ in. longer at top than C-C.

The pocket facings are preferably cut on the selvedge of the cloth (as are those on the diagram marked D), as then it is not necessary to fold in the raw edge when sewing it to the pocket, and the thickness of turned edges is avoided. The facings for the side pockets are cut $7\frac{1}{4}$ x 2 in.; those for the back pocket, $6\frac{1}{4}$ x $2\frac{1}{2}$ in.

The position of the back pocket, X-X, is 3 in. below the top edge, and parallel with it. When the belt is added, this will make the pocket mouth $4\frac{1}{2}$ in. below the top edge, which is proper for average sizes. The mouths of the back pockets are to finish $5\frac{1}{4}$ in. wide.

In cutting, do not forget to nick the cloth at all points where the pattern is notched — at the knee, hip, lower fly, and each end of the mouth of the side pocket. Make certain, too, that the outseam of the backpart is the same length as the outseam of the forepart, and that the inseams of the forepart and backpart are also equal in length. Lack of care in those matters often results in twisting legs, a very serious defect in trousers. Good trouser makers always sew up the legs so that the knee nicks coincide perfectly, and also the bottoms, and the top edges.

Marking, inserting fork pieces, and overcasting the edges

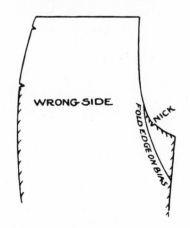

FIG. 138. Marking, inserting fork stays, and overcasting edges.

After having cut the trouser, threadmark the inlays of the backpart, and the mouth of the back pockets.

Sew the darts on the backparts and press them open.

Cut two small square pieces of lining, and fold each from point to point, doubling it into a triangle. Baste one of these triangles onto the fork of each forepart, as shown in Fig. 138, afterward trimming the edges. These pieces will act as reinforcements to the crotch.

This done, begin overcasting all raw edges to prevent their raveling. Overcast the foreparts from the fly nick clear down to the bottom of the leg; and along the other side, from the lower nick of the side pocket down to the bottom. Overcast backparts completely along both sides. This work is done with ordinary cotton thread, and the stitches taken loosely, about ½ in. apart.

Cutting the pocket pieces

Now, cut out the four pieces for the side and back pockets. Those for the side pockets will be 14 in. long and 14 in. wide, which will make them 7 in. wide folded lengthwise. Those for the back pockets will be 11 in. long by 14 in. wide, thus also 7 in. wide when folded lengthwise. Shape the pockets as suggested in Figs. 139-150.

Making the side pockets

Fig. 139. Place pant forepart right side up on the pocket, which should extend ⅜ in. at the side and ½ in. at the top. Baste from top nick to bottom nick.

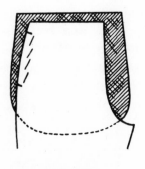

FIG. 139.

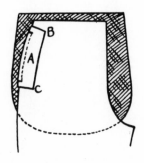

FIG. 140.

Fig. 140. Take facing piece A, which is 7¼ by 2 in. and baste it, wrong side up, in the position shown. The inside edge, B-C, is the selvedge of the cloth. Seam from nick to nick on the sewing machine.

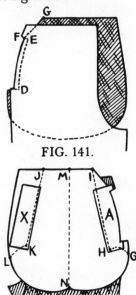

FIG. 141.

FIG. 142.

Fig. 141. Nick through all layers (at the original nicks) to permit turning in the facing. Baste facing from D to E as you turn it. Sew edge seam from D to E, and clip off pocket corner from F to G.

Fig. 142. In this figure, the forepart has been turned over to give a view of the inside of pocket. Sew the seam from G to H to I, joining the facing to the pocket. Take the other facing piece, X, and so place it that when pocket is folded in center at M-N the facing X will lie congruent on the facing A. Sew the seam J to K to L, as suggested.

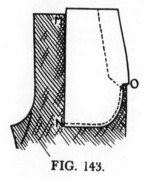

FIG. 143.

Fig. 143. Fold the pocket wrong side out on its center line, M-N, and seam from O around to N. Trim and turn pocket right side out, and sew another seam from O to N from the outside, as shown.

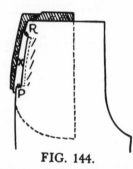

FIG. 144.

Fig. 144. Here the forepart is viewed again from the outside. Baste down mouth of pocket, going through all layers. Then fasten forepart corners P and R to the facing, X, with several hand stitches.

Temporarily, this completes the side pockets. They will be finished after the side seams are sewn.

MAKING THE BACK POCKETS

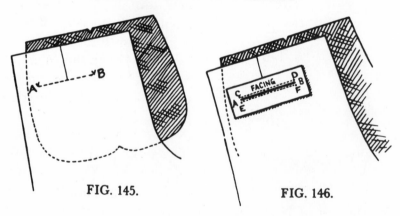

FIG. 145.

FIG. 146.

Making the back pockets

Fig. 145. Baste the trouser backpart right side up, upon the pocket, as shown. The lower edge of the pocket should be 6¾ in. below the pocket mouth, so that the finished pocket will be 6½ in. deep. The side edge of pocket outside of A is 1 in.

Fig. 146. Baste the facing right side down onto the pocket mouth, A-B, the lower edge of the facing being the selvedge of the cloth. Sew the seam C-D through all layers, ⅛ in. above line A-B; sew, also, the seam E-F ⅛ in. below A-B. Cut between seams along line A-B — through facing, trouser, and pocket.

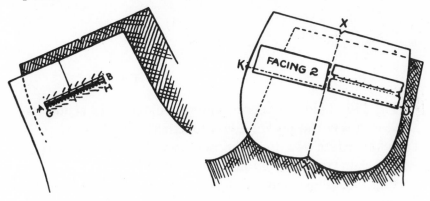

FIG. 147.   FIG. 148.

Fig. 147. Turn in the facing through the cut A-B, basting along the edges as you turn them. Do not turn in the facing entirely out of sight — its edge should show as a narrow, even piping ⅛ in. wide. This done, close the pocket mouth with loose basting stitches.

Take a machine seam along the lower edge, from G to H, binding all layers together. Leave thread ends so that they may be passed through the cloth, and tied on the reverse side.

Fig. 148. Depicts the backpart turned over, showing the inside of the pocket. As the ends of the facing curl up after being turned in, grasp each end, pulling it outward as you iron it down flat. Baste facing 2 on the other side of the pocket, and machine-sew from J to K, fastening the bottom edge of both facings to the pocket.

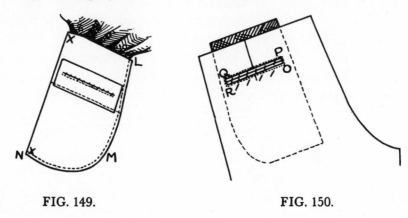

FIG. 149.   FIG. 150.

Fig. 149. Fold the pocket wrong side out on its center line X-X, and sew the pocket edges together from L to M to N. Trim the edges and turn the pocket right side out. Take a second seam from the outside around edge L-M-N.

Fig. 150. This figure shows the backpart right side out again.

Baste the pocket mouth in proper position onto the pocket, and sew a seam through all layers from O to P, continuing across to Q, then down to R. A bar-tack made at each end of the pocket mouth will complete the back pocket.

Taking the side seams

After the side and back pockets are made, the foreparts may be joined to the backparts by sewing the outside seams of the legs. The beginner had better baste the backparts to the foreparts before taking these long side seams on the machine. Make certain that the nicks at the knee and hip coincide, so that the leg will hang clean and straight. At S, it is necessary to cut ⅝ in. deep through the *underlayer* of the pocket in order to be able to press the side seam open. The cut is made about ¼ in.

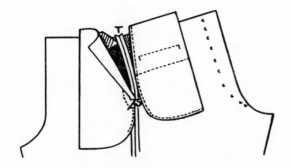

FIG. 151. Taking the Side Seams.

below the pocket bar-tack and points downward diagonally, as shown. Both the facing and pocketing are cut through, but, as only the underlayer of the pocket is thus treated, the cut does not show and does not weaken the pocket. Fig. 151 shows the side seams sewn and pressed open.

Making the belt loops

You may now make the belt loops.

Eight belt loops are required on a well-made trouser; one at each side directly behind the side seam, one at the center of each forepart, one at the center of each backpart, one at the center-back seam, and one on the right forepart, 2 in. from the fly seam.

Fold the strips for the loops wrong side out, lengthwise, and sew along the raw edge on the machine, producing a small tube. Then, with a crochet needle or something similar, pull the tube inside out and press it flat. Sew a finish seam along each side of it, and cut each 10 in. length into four loops. You will have eight strong loops in all.

In placing the loops, you may be guided by chalk marks previously measured off, but it is not necessary that they be located with absolute precision. The loop at the center back will not be put on until the trousers are closed at the center-back seam.

CONSTRUCTING THE FLY AND TOP

As trousers are commonly made to close with slide fasteners, or "zippers," a procedure especially suited to beginners for constructing such a fly is given in the instructions that follow.

The easiest method that I have found in my work with students is to first attach the zipper to the *right* forepart (or leg) of the trouser, as shown in Figs. 152-156. In fact, it will no doubt be helpful to construct most of the right leg before joining it to the left leg.

This means that the inseams of both legs should be stitched. Therefore, first of all, lay the edge of the forepart inseam against the threadmarks of the backpart inseam, being careful that the nicks at the knees coincide. Baste the inseam from the top to the bottom of the leg, stitch it on the machine, and press it open. Stitch the inseams of both legs this way, so that both are tubes before you commence construction of the fly.

For most trousers, a heavy zipper, 11 in. in length, is used. If too long, as it generally is, it may be cut at the top, slightly above the seam, B, Fig. 154.

The following series of figures do not show the trouser legs as tubes, but you must bear in mind that they are, as both the outseam and inseam have been stitched.

Attaching zipper to right forepart

Fig. 152. This shows the right trouser leg, right side out, with both the outseam and the inseam stitched and pressed open, point A being the front notch. First, baste the zipper along the front edge, beginning at A and going up to B. In starting, you will have placed the little metal

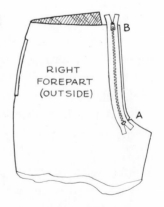

RIGHT FOREPART (OUTSIDE)

B

A

FIG. 152.

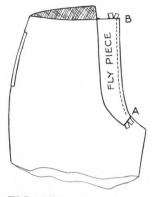

FIG. 153.

FIG. 154.

bar of the zipper a bit above A; baste neither tight nor loose, but in between.

Fig. 153. Next, place the cloth fly piece directly over the zipper, as here shown, and baste it also from A to B. Machine-stitch from B to A, stitching through the fly piece, zipper edge, and forepart edge.

Fig. 154. Press open seam A-B and open the zipper as shown here. Baste the waistband to the trouser top all around, starting on the right side of the trouser at X, but on the left side at D. Baste while holding the trouser top edge *onto* the waistband, in order that the waistband will be a bit shorter all around than the trouser top. As you baste, insert ends of belt loops in the seam, at sides, mid-backs, and mid-fronts.

Machine-stitch the waistband onto the right side of the trouser from X to D and onto the left side from D to X. Always place the waistband topmost on the machine so that the machine will automatically "full in" the trouser top edge onto the waistband. Again, on the right side, machine-stitch from X to D and on the left side from D to X.

Do not concern yourself as yet with the watch pocket, but stitch the waistband clear across the right forepart.

Fig. 155(a). Cut a flap lining out of heavy pocketing material in the shape of the right fly piece, but 1¼ in. wider and with a "tail" at the base 1¼ in. wide by 3 in. long.

141

Fig. 155(b). Baste the flap lining just cut onto the right fly piece, as A to B to C, trim the edges, and machine-stitch from C to B to A.

Fig. 156. Then turn the flap lining inside the fly piece and baste the edge as shown, from A to B to C. (This figure still shows the right front of the trouser, but viewed from the inside.) Also turn the inner edge of the flap lining piece, basting it onto the fly seam, as from E to F. Above F, the edge should be left unbasted for inserting the waistband canvases later. Below E, each side of the "tail" is folded and pressed.

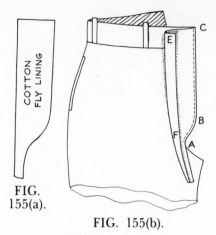

FIG. 155(a).

FIG. 155(b).

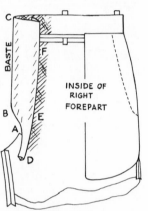

FIG. 156.

Making the Watch Pocket

At this point, you may interrupt the work on the fly to make the watch pocket. This is generally made on the right forepart and must be constructed before putting in the waistband canvases.

Fig. 157. Cut a piece of pocketing on the length of the cloth, about 4 x 8 in. Baste one end of this pocket piece on the belt seam from inside the trouser, as shown. Then, from the outside of the trouser, sew seam C-D just below the seam of the belt. The width of the pocket mouth is usually 3 in.

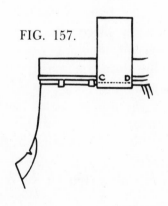

FIG. 157.

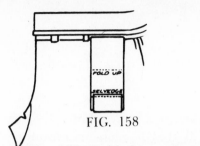

FIG. 158

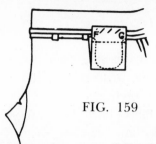

FIG. 159

Fig. 158. Fold down the pocketing on the seam C-D. On the other end of the pocketing, sew a cloth facing 4 x 2 in., seaming along the selvedge side.

Fig. 159. Fold up the pocket piece so that the facing end covers the belt seam, and baste it thus. Then sew on the machine from F around to G, forming the pocket. Finally, overcast by hand or by machine along the raw edges of the pocket to prevent raveling.

Attaching zipper to left forepart

First, baste on the waistband, placing the loops where they belong as you did on the right side. Then machine-stitch the waistband.

Fig. 160(a). Now, using the remaining fly piece as a pattern, cut a piece of wigan to its shape but a bit narrower. Place the fly piece onto the left forepart as from E to F; place the wigan directly onto it; and baste both the fly piece and wigan onto the forepart, E to F. Machine-stitch from E to F, F being a point about 1 in. below the top (in order to leave the seam open there to permit later stitching of the fly piece extension). The wigan adds body to the finished fly.

Figure 160(b). Turn in and baste the fly piece from E to F and press.

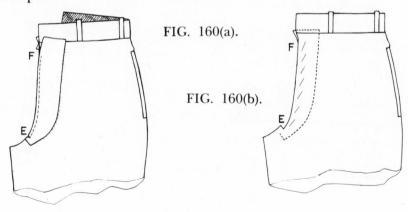

FIG. 160(a).

FIG. 160(b).

143

At this stage in constructing a trouser with a zipper fly, we cannot proceed further without joining the legs together at the crotch.

Place both legs together at the crotch, matching the fly nicks and starting your basting at the fly nicks, continuing toward the back of the trouser to a point just above the curve of the seat. Then machine-stitch the legs together from the fly nick into the seat, a distance of about 8 in. (You should not stitch clear to the top of the trouser at the back because you have no means of measuring for the correct waist size until the fly is finished.) You are now ready to fasten the zipper to the left side, or leg.

Fig. 161. First, baste the left forepart edge onto the right forepart as from E to F, making sure that the tops coincide at F and that the zipper is concealed by the overlapping left forepart about ⅜ in. Baste along the edge only, the aim being to close the fronts as they should close in the finished garment.

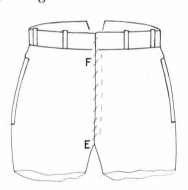

FIG. 161.

Fig. 162(a). Turn trouser inside out as shown in this diagram. Turn over fly flap X toward the right and out of the way. Baste zipper to fly piece Y from G to H. Machine-stitch from G to H, running the first stitching along the middle of the zipper tape and a second stitching along its outer edge. These stitchings run through the fly piece only, of course, and do not go through the outer trouser.

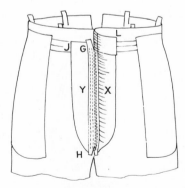

FIG. 162(a).

144

Fig. 162(b). Cut a small, square piece of cloth, the fly piece extension which is Z in Fig. 163(a), about 2¾ x 2¾ in., and machine-stitch it from J to K, running through the zipper at G. Press open seam J-K. Cut

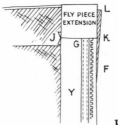

FIG. 162(b).

the zipper end about ⅜ in. above the seam, and press it upward. Finally, machine-stitch from K to L.

Basting in waistband canvases

Waistband canvases may be made of heavy cotton drilling, or other stiff, non-stretchable material, and are cut on the length of the material about 3¼ in. wide. There must be two of them, each measuring half of the waist measurement plus 4 in.

Fig. 163(a). First baste waistband canvases along their top edges to the top of the trouser, ½″ below the waistband edge. Then baste along their lower edges, folding the canvas upwardly just below the waistband seam in order to give them a strong, frayless lower edge. Also, as you baste the bottom edge, you may insert the tops of the pockets under the canvas.

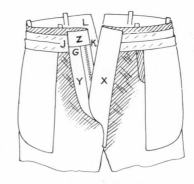

FIG. 163(a).

At the front top corners of the fly on each side, as at L, trim the canvases ⅜ in. inside the waistband edge and trim their corners a bit rounded.

Fig. 163(b). The top edges of the trouser are now folded down ½ in. onto the canvas top and then hand-stitched to

FIG. 163(b).

it with fairly wide stitches. The tops of the fly piece and lining, L-M-N and O-P-Q, are also folded in and hand-stitched with the corners, L and O, rounded a bit. The ends of the waistband loops are then machine-stitched to the top edge, turned over inside the trouser, and hand-stitched to the canvas, as shown.

FIG. 164.

FIG. 165.

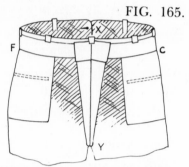

Fig. 164. A neat machine-stitching should now be run from the outside of the trouser. This is best done by turning the trouser inside out and starting the stitching on the left forepart at the base of the fly, A. Stitch in a gentle curve up to B, then continuing under and close to the waistband seam to C, and around to the back at D.

On the right side, start machine-stitching at E, continuing in the same fashion to F and G. Then run the seam up to G, which is just above the seam of the watch pocket. Continue stitching just *above* and along the seam to H, then down again to J, to K, and down to L.

This figure also shows where the buttonholes are cut, one on the left forepart in the center of the waistband and about ½ or ⅝ in. from its front edge, the other on the fly flap, just about ⅜ in. below the waistband seam and ½ in. inside the front edge.

Fig. 165. The waist may now be measured to the wearer's actual waist measurement. This is done by folding the trouser waist on the double, much as shown in this figure, and measuring with the tape from F to C. This measurement multiplied by 2 will give you the actual waist measure of the trouser as now basted, and you may proceed to chalk-line the back seam, X-Y, with such addition or reduction as is necessary to obtain the proper waist measure of the wearer.

FINISHING THE TROUSER

Machine-stitch the center-back seam through your chalk-line *twice* as this seam must be especially strong to withstand the strain over the seat. Indeed, good tailors run a third stitching with heavy silk, by hand, in the crotch and lower seat. Trim the inlay to 1¾ in. wide each side at the top, narrowing the inlay width as it goes down. Press open the center-back seam from the waistband to the fly nick. Hand-stitch the inlay top corners to the waistband canvas, and machine-stitch the center-back loop.

Finish the corners of the fly by hand. Overcast the raw edge of the fly piece, stitching it at the top to the waistband canvas. Overcast any other raw edge that is left inside the trouser to prevent ravelling.

Place the "tail" of the fly lining onto the crotch seam, and hand-stitch it to that seam along both sides with heavy button thread. Examine a pair of ready-made trousers to see how the tail is sewn.

Take a length of heavy buttonhole silk thread that matches the trouser, rub it with beeswax, and pass it under the warm iron so that it will be stiff and gnarl-proof. Turn the trouser right side out and make a bar-tack just above the fly nick. This tack is often made in the shape of a small triangle, instead of a straight bar, with "through" stitches joining firmly all layers at the base point of the fly.

Turn in the back edges of the side pockets, which you remember were left loose (Fig. 151), and fell these edges neatly to the side seams with white silk.

Take another length of heavy silk that you used for making the fly bar-tack, and make bar-tacks also at both ends of the mouths of each pocket. Make the tacks strong and have the stitches show as little as possible inside the trouser—mere dots if possible. Even though the mouth of the watch pocket is, for the time, stitched closed, make strong bar-tacks at each of its ends. After the pants have been pressed, you will open the watch pocket by carefully cutting open the seam with a small knife.

Finally, cut and make the two buttonholes, one through the front top corner of the waistband on the left forepart, the other through the fly flap on the right forepart directly below the waistband seam, Fig. 164.

If the fly has been properly made, the top edges of both sides should lie evenly on each other. Frequently, beginners will stretch one side longer than the other, which results in uneven tops. This is something to guard against as you construct this section.

Sewing in the waist lining

The next operation is to sew in the waist lining, as shown in Figs. 166(a) and 166(b).

Cut the waist lining out of sateen or other durable material. Cut across the width of the material a strip 3 in. wide. Lay it on the canvas, wrong side up, as shown in Fig. 166(a), and begin stitching it by hand to the lower edge of canvas at A. At the center back, make a little fold, or tuck, so there will be extra material there should it become necessary to enlarge the waist.

Having stitched the lower edge of the lining, throw it over upward, basting it in place all around. Then finely hand-stitch the upper edge onto the trouser top edge, as shown in Fig. 166(b).

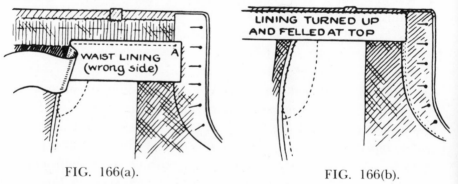

FIG. 166(a).   FIG. 166(b).

Making the cuffs

Cuffs may be made only after the trousers are pressed.

Lay the trouser on its side, pulling top leg out of the way, as shown, Fig. 167.

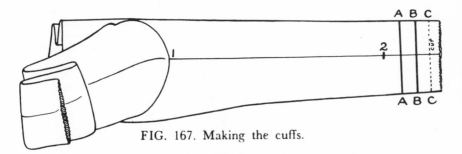

FIG. 167. Making the cuffs.

2 from 1 is the inseam measure. Make a chalk mark at 2.

Draw line A-A, 1¾ in. below 2.

Draw line B-B, 1¾ in. below A-A.

Cut the bottom about 1½ in. below B-B, as at C-C in diagram.

Turn trouser legs inside out. Fold *in* the bottoms on line A-A, basting them loosely. Then fold *out* on line B-B, also basting them thus. Now fell the raw edge by hand all around, and tack cuff loosely on both seams, working from the inside.

NOTE: The felling is wisely postponed until after the trousers have been tried on for length, as it is difficult to predetermine the correct length by measurement.

Problems of posture and how to alter the pattern for them

PROBLEM 1, Figs. 168, 169. To determine how much the belt must be lowered at the back, pin out a horizontal fold just below the belt, as at X, Fig. 168. This fold will probably involve ¾ in. of excess to be removed at the center back, decreasing to ½ in. over each pocket and decreasing to nothing at the sides. Thus pinned out, the trousers will at once hang much better, and the folds under the buttocks will have disappeared; but added width will appear in the seat region, B, Fig. 169, which must also be pinned out and removed. In Fig. 169, the black lines are the normal pattern; the dashed lines represent the changes necessary for this figure form. It is, of course, best to incorporate these changes in the pattern before making the trousers, as on a finished trouser the alteration slightly tilts the back pockets at the back end.

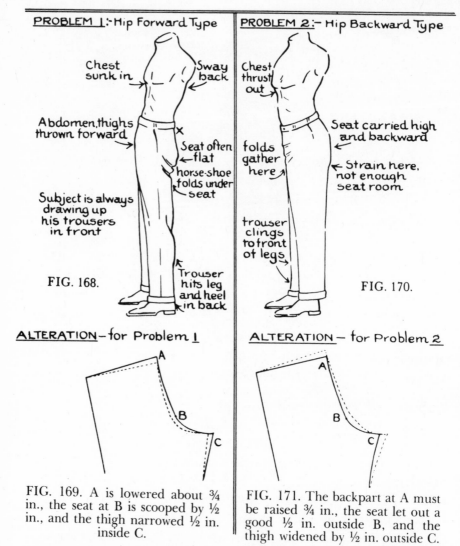

Chest sunk in

Sway back

Abdomen, thighs thrown forward →

Seat often ←flat

horse-shoe folds under seat

Subject is always drawing up his trousers in front

FIG. 168.

Trouser hits leg and heel in back

ALTERATION–for Problem 1

A

B

C

FIG. 169. A is lowered about ¾ in., the seat at B is scooped by ½ in., and the thigh narrowed ½ in. inside C.

PROBLEM 2:- Hip Backward Type

Chest thrust out

Seat carried high and backward ←

← Strain here, not enough seat room

folds gather here ↗

trouser clings to front of legs ↘

FIG. 170.

ALTERATION — for Problem 2

A

B

C

FIG. 171. The backpart at A must be raised ¾ in., the seat let out a good ½ in. outside B, and the thigh widened by ½ in. outside C.

PROBLEM 2, Figs. 170, 171. This type is not so common as the hip-forward type, and, in any case, nothing much can be done about it after the trousers are made. The problem is the converse of Problem 1. In drafting the pattern, raise the back point ½ in. to ¾ in. above A, Fig. 171, and widen the back outside B, ½ in. on the half pattern. Add also ½ in. outside C. These changes will provide extra latitude and longitude in the seat region, and added width to the thigh.

Reducing trousers in seat and thigh

Trousers do not usually require other altering than some slight reduction in the back seam. If cut a bit on the large side, their fitting presents no problem at all.

When the waist section is too large but the seat is right, the back seam is taken in only at the top, the amount removed gradually decreasing to nothing in the seat region. In this case, a *wedge* of excess is removed rather than an even strip.

But when trousers must be reduced in the seat, they usually must be reduced in the thigh, and to the same extent. Thus, if the half pattern is reduced 1 in. inside A, Fig.

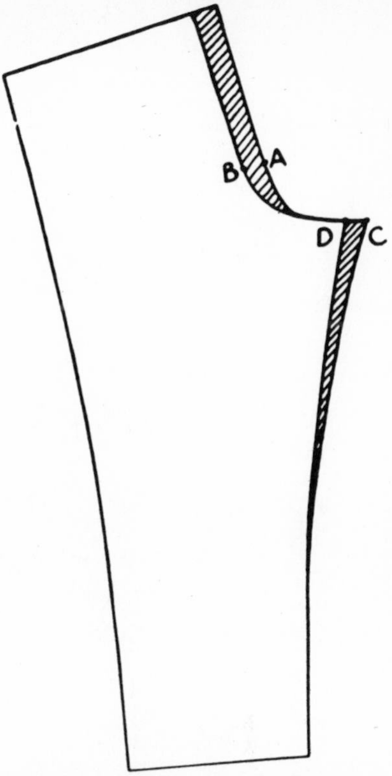

FIG. 172. Reducing trousers in seat and thigh. If a trouser must be reduced in the seat, as from A to B, it must usually be reduced an equal amount in the thigh, C to D.

172, it must also be reduced 1 in. inside C—else an unsightly blob will appear below the round of buttocks. Only when the individual is unusually heavily built in the seat and thighs is it unnecessary to reduce the thigh.

Pressing

Press a newly made trouser first from the inside, ironing the pockets and whatever seams have not been opened. Then turn it right side out, and press around the top, rotating it on the end of the sleeveboard as you work. Next, lay the left leg flat on the bench as in Fig. 167, placing the inseam directly upon the outseam and pressing it thus from the inside leg. In like manner, press the right leg. Then, laying the left leg on the right, press the left leg from the outside. In like manner, press right leg from the outside.

Chapter IX

Vest Making

THE VEST as worn nowadays is commonly sleeveless, collarless, and cut with widened armholes. It has four welt pockets and six buttons.

FIG. 173. Two examples of vests cut on the formula of FIG. 175. Note the run of the stitching at the pocket corners of the vest at the left. The tartan vest, right, requires painstaking matching of the pocket welts, revers, and lower flapped pockets, but the effort is always rewarded with a very attractive garment.

It is not a difficult garment to make, requiring approximately six hours from cutting to finishing; and the measurements used and the method of fitting are the same as those utilized for the coat. Indeed, the vest is a short, sleeveless coat, and the English do very aptly term it waist-coat.

The materials for making a vest are: rayon lining—enough to cut out the outer back and the belt pieces; wigan — enough to cover the foreparts; silesia — enough for four pockets; sateen lining of good quality — enough to cut out the inner back and the two linings for the foreparts; staytape — enough to go around the edges of both foreparts; a buckle for the belt (if a belt at the back is desired) ; and six buttons of No. 24 size.

Measurements for a vest

The measurements required for drafting a vest are: (1) *Length of vest back;* (2) *chest* (over shirt); (3) *waist;* (4) *vest front length,* from nape of neck down to the point at bottom of front; and (5) *vest opening,* from nape of neck down to the topmost button at front. How to measure the vest length and opening is shown in Fig. 174.

THE VEST FORMULA (See Page 155)

Chest, 42 in.	Vest opening, 15 in.
Chest scale, 21 in.	Vest front length, 29 in.
Waist 36 in.	Vest back length, 22 in.

2 from 1 is $\frac{1}{2}$ chest scale plus 1 in. ($11\frac{1}{2}$ in., in this case).

3 is midway between 2 and 1.

4 is midway between 3 and 1.

5 from 1 is the waist depth, or $\frac{1}{4}$ total height of subject.

6 from 1 is the vest back length, plus $\frac{1}{2}$ in. for seams ($22\frac{1}{2}$ in.).

7 from 2 is $\frac{1}{3}$ chest scale plus $\frac{1}{4}$ in. ($7\frac{1}{4}$ in.). Square up.

8 from 2 is $\frac{1}{2}$ in.

A from 5 is $1\frac{1}{4}$ in. Rule from A to 8, and from 8 to 4.

B from 1 is $\frac{1}{6}$ chest scale plus $\frac{1}{4}$ in., and $\frac{7}{8}$ in. above the top line.

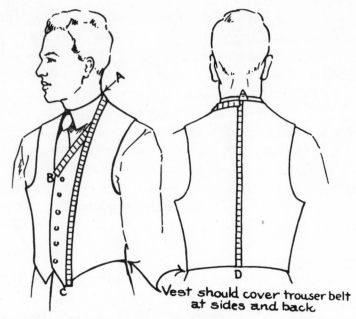

FIG. 174. Measurements for a vest. Vest opening: measure from A, the nape of neck, to B, the position of the top button. Vest front length: measure from A, to C, the point of vest bottom. Vest back length: measure from A to the lower seam of the belt, at D. Proportionate rule: vest opening is ordinarily half of the vest front length.

C is 1 in. below the top line, and rule line B-C.

9 from 8 is ⅔ chest scale (14 in.). Square down.

10^1 from 8 is the chest scale plus 2½ in. (23½ in.). Square down.

11 is midway between 9 and 10^1. Square up, locating 13.

12 below 13 is ⅞ in. for a normal figure, 1½ in. for a stooped figure. For an erect figure, point 12 rises close to point 13.

10^2 is ½ in. above 10^1. Rule from 10^2 to 12.

Place the elbow of the square on point 12, and square out by line 12-10^2 to D^1. D^2 is ½ in. above D^1.

D^2 from 12 is the same as C from B.

F is 1¾ in. inside E. Curve armhole all around as suggested.

16 from 9 is 1¾ in. Square down to X.

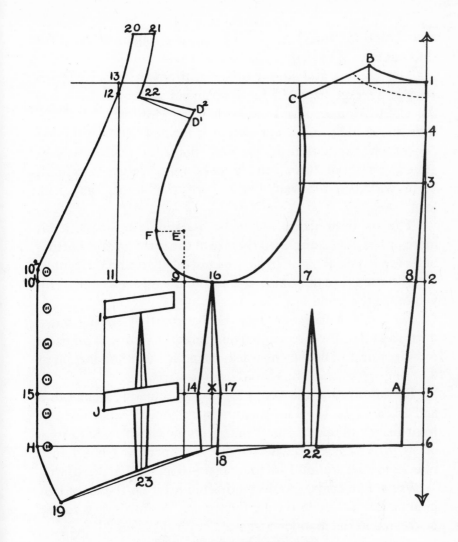

FIG. 175. The Vest Formula.

14 from X is ¾ in. Rule from 16 to 14.

17 from X is ½ in. Rule from 16 to 17, dropping to 18 which is ¼ in. below the bottom line.

19 from H is ⅙ chest scale. Rule from 19 to the bottom line above 18. Shape the point of the bottom as suggested.

The dashed line below the top of the back is ¾ in. below line B-1. Cut the pattern through this dotted line. The strip added onto the forepart, 12-20-21-22, is a replica of the piece thus cut out. This strip is $1\frac{1}{4}$ in. wide.

The pockets at I and J are 4 in. from the front edge in vests of average size; $4\frac{1}{4}$ in. in large vests. I is $2\frac{1}{2}$ in. below the chestline, and J is 1 in. below the waistline. When the waistline is high, the lower pocket is located between the top pocket and the bottom of the vest. Slant the pockets as suggested; a slant of $\frac{3}{4}$ in. usually looks well. Welts are to finish $\frac{7}{8}$ in. wide; the top welt, $4\frac{1}{2}$ in. long; the bottom welt, 5 in. long.

The six buttonholes are to be marked 2 in. apart, a bit more or less in keeping with the size of the vest. Eyes of buttonholes are to be cut $\frac{1}{2}$ in. from the finished edge, and the centers of the buttons are to be also $\frac{1}{2}$ in. from the finished edge. This will make the fronts lap 1 in.

For small waists, suppress the backpart by sewing out a dart, as at 22. If more suppression is required, due to an extra full chest or a hollow front waist, introduce another dart, as at 23. In general, however, avoid cutting darts.

Having drafted the vest, measure continuously from 1 to B and from 12 to 19. This measurement should equal the vest front length as taken, plus 1 in. for seams (in this vest, a total of 30 in.). Check likewise on the vest opening, from 1 to B plus 12 to 10^2, adding 1 in. for seams (16 in. total in this draft).

Vests, like coats, should be drafted a bit on the large size, pinning out the excess during the try-on. Women's vests should be treated in the manner suggested in Figs. 19 and 20.

CUTTING THE VEST

In cutting the vest foreparts, allow inlays about 1 in. wide along the front and the bottom, as in Fig. 176. Threadmark along the front and bottom and at each end of the pocket mouths.

The facings for the front and bottom edges are cut from the cloth in the shape suggested in Fig. 177. The material used for the linings of both forepart and backpart is generally a fine

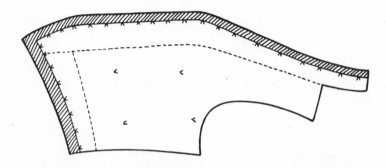

FIG. 176. Cutting the vest fronts. Inlays are provided along the front edge and the bottom. Dashed lines indicate how the pattern may be divided to cut the facings and linings as shown below, Fig. 177.

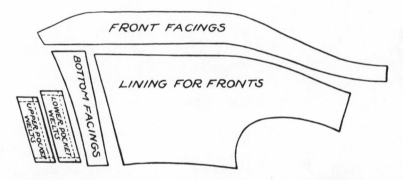

FIG. 177. Cutting the facings and linings for the vest foreparts. Front and bottom facings are cut from the cloth; lining for fronts is of sateen.

sateen of pearl or ivory color. The forepart lining should be cut rather large as it requires seam allowances all around and needs to be put in loosely.

The outer backpart is cut from the same matching rayon as was used to line the suit coat. Inlays are allowed along the sides and bottom, only. The backpart lining is cut in the exact shape of the outer backpart, inlays included. Threadmark only the outer backpart, however; the backpart lining needs no threadmarking.

Cut two belt pieces, also out of the rayon, 3 in. wide at one end, 2 in. at the other, and longer than the width of the half-back (17-A, Fig. 175) by about 2 in.

Preparing the backpart

To prepare the back, first sew the halves together and press the seam open. Do this with the lining back as with the outer back.

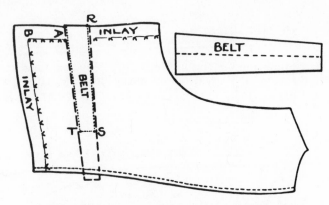

FIG. 178. Cutting and preparing the backparts.

Now fold the belt pieces lengthwise, wrong side out, and seam them along the cut edge and clear around the smaller end. With the help of the bodkin, turn the tube so formed right side out, and press it flat. Thus finished, it will be ¾ in. wide at the small end and 1¼ in. wide at the wide end. Lay these belt halves with their lower edges about 3¼ in. above bottom of back, their small ends extending ¼ in. beyond the center-back seam. Sew them to the back from R to S, S being about 4 in. from center back; then across to T, and beyond A to edge.

Basting up for the try-on

Fig. 179. Cut two lengths of wigan in the shape of the vest forepart, but a little larger all around. Lay each forepart onto one of these, and baste flat on the bench, first down the center, then along each side within 1¼ in. from the edges. Trim the wigan all around the edges of the foreparts.

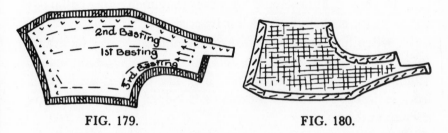

FIG. 179. FIG. 180.

Fig. 180. Lay the foreparts wrong side up on the bench and trim the wigan around the armhole, about ⅜ in. inside the edge of the cloth. Nick the cloth at intervals around the curve of the armhole to permit its being turned. Turn-in the width of a seam all around the armhole, basting neatly. Turn-in the inlays along the vest front and bottom, ¼ in. inside the thread-marks.

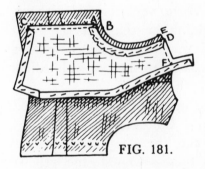

FIG. 181.

Fig. 181. Lay the left fore-part on the backpart, the back-part edge at B extending one seam outside of A, and the side of the forepart lying against the threadmarks on the back-part. Baste from A to C. Treat the right forepart in the same manner.

Lay the shoulder of vest forepart onto the backpart. Have the back edge, E, extend a full seam outside D. Baste shoulder from D to F.

Having basted up both foreparts to the back, join the two neck strips together at the back neck with a few loose basting stitches.

The vest is now ready to try on.

THE TRY-ON—FITTING OF VEST

Vests are subject to the same defects of balance as are coats, and lend themselves to the same corrections. Therefore, in fitting vests, apply the methods demonstrated in Figs. 34-44.

The vest neckline should not cover too much of the collar — above ½ in. is enough. The left front should lap 1 in. over the right, when finished. The finished vest should be of a length to cover the trouser belt at sides and back — never so long that it covers the tops of the trouser pockets. The point at the bottom front is best made rather short, as a too-long point has a tendency to curl up.

Buttons are planned to be about 2 in. apart; and on a very small vest, they may be five in number instead of the conventional six.

Pocket position is important, and in trying-on it is well for the tailor to chalk the outline of the welts on the cloth to judge if they are correctly located.

Making of vest pockets

Having tried on and corrected the vest, rip the foreparts from the back preparatory to building the welt pockets.

Vest pockets are cut and built much in the same way as is the outside breast pocket of the coat. But the vest welt differs from the coat welt in the following features:

(1) The front corners of the vest welts are not rounded as in the coat welt, but are folded in almost a square point.

(2) The vest welts are sewn onto the silesia pieces by machine, instead of the silesia being hand-sewn onto the welt, as in the coat.

(3) Once joined to the vest, the welt is sewn around the corners also by machine, but the tack is run in the shape of a small parallelogram, Fig. 183.

Cut and make the welts in the manner shown in Figs. 68 and 69, Chapter VII. The top pocket welts are to be 4½ in. long when finished; the bottom pocket welts, 5 in. long. The width of the finished welts is ⅞ in. The top pockets are to finish 6 in. deep; the bottom pockets, 5 in. deep, or a bit less.

Fig. 182. Machine-sew the welts onto the silesia pieces, leaving the thread ends long either side, so that they may be drawn from the reverse and tied. Notch out the corners of the silesia pieces as shown in Fig. 70, and sew the welts onto the vest foreparts as in Figs. 71 and 72.

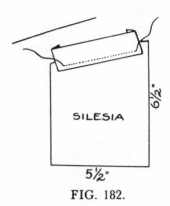

FIG. 182.

Fig. 183. In sewing the welt ends on the machine, start the seams as at A and make the two vertical seams of the tack $\frac{5}{16}$ in. apart. Again, leave the thread ends long so that they

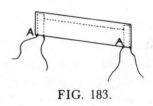

FIG. 183.

may be drawn and tied from behind. Having done this, trim the edges of the silesias and sew around them to form the inside pocket.

JOINING FACINGS TO LININGS

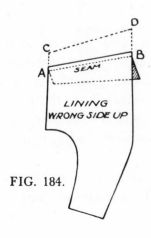

FIG. 184.

Fig. 184. Having finished and pressed the pockets, proceed to join the facings to the linings of the foreparts.

Machine-sew the left forepart lining onto the bottom facing, as from A to B. Turn the facing outward, as at C to D. Similarly, sew the right forepart lining to its bottom facing.

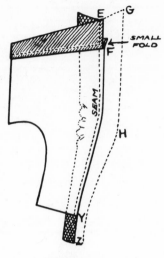

FIG. 185.

Fig. 185. Now sew the left forepart lining onto the front facing, beginning the seam at E. Make a small fold in the lining at the junction of the bottom facing, F, and sew through this fold. Its function is to prevent the lining from becoming too short as a result of shrinkage. Continue the seam up to the top, Y, and turn the facing outward, as at G-H, pressing open the seam from E to F.

In making up the facing for the right forepart, sew the forepart lining onto the facing beginning the seam from the top, as at Y. (Linings must always be uppermost in sewing on the machine.) The starting point, Y, on the right facing is located by measuring from Z the same distance that Y is from Z on the left forepart facing.

Finally, neatly press the facings and linings all over.

You are now ready to start making the fronts.

Making up the fronts

To simplify the task of exposition here, the making of the right forepart only is considered.

Take the right forepart and lay it right side up on the bench. Then lay onto it the front facing (for that forepart) right side down. Begin basting on the facing at the point of bottom, continuing up along the front edge. Baste the facing on fair until you get to the topmost button, beyond which you should ease in a bit of fullness, as a too-short facing must be avoided at all costs.

Now, baste the bottom facing fair along the vest bottom. Then hold up the vest by the shoulder to make sure that the lining falls fair and a bit loosely over the vest front. If it falls satisfactorily thus, the chances are it will also do so when turned out.

Take the staytape and begin basting it along the edge, starting 2½ in. below the shoulder line, as it is undesirable to have the edge drawn in the gorge section of the finished garment. Baste the staytape ³⁄₁₆ in. inside the front edge, and lay it just a trifle short (lengthwise) along the button edge and just a bit shorter above the top button and along the bottom edge. Baste it in the same manner as you were instructed for coats, and hand-fell its inside edge to the wigan with wide, loose stitches.

After the tape has been basted, press it flat, using very little moisture to avoid stretching it and being careful to retain the breast shape that the drawn-in edge is meant to impart to the vest front.

Now take the edge seam on the machine, sewing along and through the outer edge of the tape. Begin the seam at the bottom, sewing from the side to the bottom point, then up toward the shoulder to within 1½ in. of the end of the neck strip. You will be sewing through both layers of cloth, plus the wigan and the tape. This done, trim the seam even, especially close around the point of the bottom, and turn the forepart right side out.

Baste the edges all around, turning them neat and straight. Then run a second basting around the vest forepart, about 1½ in. inside the edge, curling it inward as you baste.

Lay the forepart, lining side up, on the bench and baste the lining loosely along the side of the forepart and around the armhole. Again, much care must be taken to retain some looseness in the lining, as the finished front must not be contracted in any way by the action of the too narrow lining.

Trim the lining ⅜ in. outside the run of the armhole edge, nick the lining edge at intervals, and turn it in ⅛ in. inside the armhole edge, basting all around. Machine-sew the lining thus to the armhole edge, a close finish seam around the hole.

This completes the right forepart except for the finish stitching around the edge. The left forepart is done in the same way except that the inside seam around the edge is taken from top to bottom instead of from bottom to top. For clearness' sake, I have here described all the operations as if making one front at the time; but in actual practice, both fronts are worked together, alternating the operations.

Putting on the back

You are now ready to join the foreparts to the back.

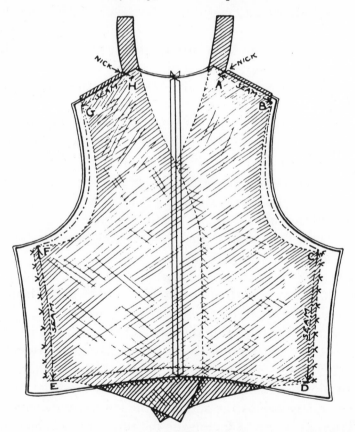

FIG. 186. Putting on the back. The vest foreparts are shown basted, or "bagged" between the backparts. The seam is started at A, following the dot-dash line all around, A-B-C-D-E-F-G-H. All layers are nicked at H and A.

Lay the outer back on the bench, right side up. Baste the left forepart lying against the threadmarks on the back, as shown in Fig. 181. In the same way, baste the right forepart to the back. Finally baste the shoulders closed, as you did for the try-on.

Lay the vest on the bench as in Fig. 186, the foreparts lining side up and lapping over each other as shown. Now take the back lining and place it right side down, onto the vest. Baste the back lining congruent onto the outer back, first along the sides and shoulders, "sandwiching" the vest foreparts between the two backs. This done, baste the backs together, congruently, around the armholes.

The foreparts of the vest being thus "bagged-in" between the two backs, proceed to take the long seam all around.

Place the vest on the sewing machine with the outer back uppermost and start stitching at the neck point A, Fig. 186. Follow the dot-dash line, which is $\frac{1}{4}$ in. inside the edge, to B; then around the armhole to C; next along the side $\frac{1}{4}$ in. inside the threadmarks, to D. In seaming along the bottom from D to E, the points of the foreparts must, of course, be turned up between the backs. Finally, continue up to F, G, and H as indicated.

After the long seam is taken, trim the excess lining around the armholes, and nick-in several places around their curves, so they may be turned in without puckering. Also, nick the shoulder points $\frac{1}{4}$ in. deep as at A and H; after which, remove all bastings from the back.

Now, thrust the hand through the neck opening, between the backs, and pull the vest foreparts out, thus turning the vest right side out. The vest is now completely assembled except for the neck section.

Finishing

The neck strips are now measured along the neckline of the outer back, and each strip is cut $\frac{1}{4}$ in. beyond the center-back seam; after which the ends are seamed together, and the seam pressed open. Then the neck strips are seamed lengthwise and finished continuous with the front edges. Both the outer back and the lining back are trimmed around the neck ½ in. below the finished edge, turned-in an additional ¼ in., and neatly felled by hand either side.

Finally, a finish stitching is run around the edges of both foreparts in one continuous seam, and the buttonholes are cut 2 in. apart.

Much of the procedure in vest making must be developed by the individual himself, who will automatically discover methods of working conducive to better order and speed. Here I have not concerned myself with presenting operations from the standpoint of speed or best order, but have adopted the simplest style of exposition in order not to confuse the beginner.

Chapter X

Skirt Making

MEASUREMENTS FOR A SKIRT

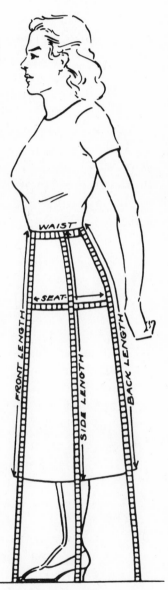

FIG. 187. Measuring for a skirt.

T HE MEASUREMENTS required for designing a skirt are five in number: (1) *waist;* (2) *seat;* (3) *front length;* (4) *side length;* and (5) *back length.*

The waist measurement is taken neither tight nor loose but in between. The seat measurement, however, is taken rather loosely around the largest part of the hips, but with as much accuracy as possible as it determines the size of the pattern. Experience here is the only teacher, but it is always best to err on the large side rather than to cut a too-small pattern and skirt.

To measure the side, front, and back lengths accurately, tie a 1¼ in. wide belt snugly around your subject's waist. Measure from the top edge of the belt down to the floor, deducting the distance the skirt is to be worn from the floor. Let us say that the front length to the floor is 42½ in., and the skirt is to be worn 12½ in. from the floor. The front length of the finished skirt would then be 30 in.

The side length of the skirt will usually measure ½ in. longer than the front length; the back length will usually measure ½ in. more than the side length. But these are only general rules, as posture and size of hips introduce a good deal of variation. With certain subjects, in fact, the back length may be less than the front length.

The hem circumference (or all-around length of the bottom) is a matter of individual taste and may be decided by measuring one of the skirts your subject has been wearing.

In this chapter, I present a draft formula for a plain skirt which is easy to understand and to follow and yet produces a garment of excellent proportions in which one might introduce many variations. I do not believe that the learner could find any system on which she could rely as well; indeed, once she knows this method, she need not cut individual patterns at all but may draft the skirt directly on the cloth.

As will be noted, the skirt is here constructed on a simple oblong with a width one-fourth of the seat measure and a length which is the actual front length of the skirt. There are no slanting lines in the formula except the two essential ones which determine the "flare."

Indeed, the only problems that might arise with this method would be those resulting from the increase in flare when the skirt is made unduly short, or with the narrowed flare when it is made for an unusually tall person. I therefore advise the student to draft at the constant length of 28 in., as in this draft, adding to the skirt length or subtracting from it afterward.

The secret of cutting good skirt patterns lies mainly in taking accurate front side, and back length measurements, and knowing that the differences between these must be placed *above* the top line of the draft and never below the bottom or hem line.

Also, the width of the waist suppression darts may not always be accurately estimated in drafting, but if the waist is made a bit too large rather than too small, one can adjust the darts perfectly during the fitting of the skirt on the subject.

THE SKIRT FORMULA

Front length, 28 in.   Seat, 40 in.
Side length, 28½ in.   Waist, 30 in.
Back length, 28¾ in.

The forepart—Fig. 188(a)

Rule line A-B, making A-B the front length (28 in.). We need not subtract the waistband width, as this will provide a 1¼ in. hem allowance at the bottom.

C is 8 in. down from A.

Square out from A, B, and C.

F from C is ¼ seat measure plus ¼ in. (10¼ in.).

E from A is the same, as is also D from B. Rule E to D to complete the oblong, A-B-D-E.

G from D is 1 in. Rule from G through F and up to J.

H from B is 1 in. Rule from H through C and up to K.

L is ⅞ in. from J. Curve down gradually from L to F.

Now, with the tape measure, measure from G up to L, the side length of the skirt (28½ in.). Or L above the top line is the difference between length of front and side measures (½ in.).

Square from H into N and from G into N. Curve the bottom line a bit above N as shown.

Curve very faintly from L into O, and cut out the entire forepart on lines H-C-K-O-L-F-G-D-N-B-H.

The dart, when one is wanted, is placed about 3¾ in. from L, and is a small ½ in. at the mouth and 3 in. long vertically.

L from K is ideally ¼ waist measure plus 1 in.

The backpart—Fig. 188(b)

Lay the forepart pattern just cut on another sheet of paper and draw around it, L-K-H-G.

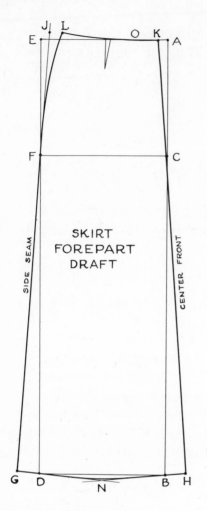

FIG. 188(a). Forepart.

FIG. 188(b). Backpart.

The Skirt Formula

WAISTBAND

3"

FIG. 189.

R from G is 1 in. Q from F is 1 in. P from L is 1¼ in. Curve the line a bit from P to Q and rule from Q to R.

P-R should measure the same as G-L.

S measured from H is the back length of the skirt (28¾ in.). Rule P to S.

Divide P-S into three equal parts, locating the darts, T and U. These darts are ½ in. wide at the mouth and 4¼ in. long vertically. Sometimes with larger waists a single back dart midway between P and S will suffice.

To compute the total that needs to be sewn out in darts, subtract the waist measure from the quantity L-K plus P-S, less 2 in. (This 2 in. is for seams and ease.) Thus, in this draft, I measure L-K plus P-S as 36½ in., which with the deduction of 2 in. comes to a total of 34½ in. Subtract from this the waist measure of 30 in., and you find that you have exactly 4½ in. of excess to take out in darts. Two-thirds of this excess should be taken out of the backpart and the remaining third out of the forepart.

The waistband, Fig. 189, is cut 3 in. wide on the length of the cloth, which permits it to fold in the middle and finish 1¼ in. wide. In length it is cut the full waist measure plus 4 in.

You may now cut the skirt backpart, S-H-R-Q-P-S.

The formula is for a two-piece skirt and has allowances for ¼-in. seams each side. Therefore, H-K and H-S should be laid on the fold edge of the cloth. If a four-piece skirt is wanted, simply add ¼ in. along H-K and H-S, and the parts will not be cut on the fold of the cloth.

Variations in figure form

I have said that the side length of a skirt is normally ½ in. longer than the front length, and that the back length is about ½ in. longer than the side. Therefore, when your measurements of a subject are close to these dimensions, you know that you are dealing with a normal or near-normal figure, and your pattern will closely resemble the draft here reproduced.

However, you will find that the relative lengths of front, side, and back often depart considerably from the norms given.

A wide-hipped woman will frequently require a side measure 1½ in. or 1¾ in. longer than the front. This will raise the point, L, on your draft so high that you will wonder if you are making a mistake. A normal skirt on such a figure will break into unsightly horizontal folds along the front of the skirt as shown in Fig. 190. Apparently this would be due to a too-long front length, but in reality it is the side length which is too short.

Frequently, also, in measuring large-buttocked figures, especially those that carry their seats far back and high, the back length will be as much as 1½ to 2 in. longer than the front length. In this case, point S will be brought way up on the draft. On such a figure, a normal skirt will flare toward the back and cling uncomfortably to the thighs at the front, where it will be much longer. This defect is illustrated in Fig. 193.

Again, you will meet figures that carry their hips forward, whose front length may be equal or longer than the back length, necessitating that point S be made coincident with point K in the draft. A normal skirt, on this type of figure, will flare outward toward the front and "cup" the buttocks, clinging to the thighs at the back and appearing much longer there, Fig. 196.

Also, you will meet with figures whose waists are extremely small in relation to their seats. Here the problem is purely one of waist suppression. More material will have to be taken out of all the darts and perhaps the side seams just below the belt.

Cutting a skirt

In cutting a skirt, leave inlays of ½ in. along each side of the foreparts and backparts. This will make your seams, as sewn, ¾ in. wide, and permit enlargement of the skirt to the extent of 1 in. in each seam.

Leave also a generous inlay at the bottom — 2½ in. wide is none too much.

The belt is preferably cut on the straight or length of the cloth; and to save cloth in a short piece, it may be cut along the fold of the cloth, thus removing only 1½ in. from the width of the folded piece. When the cloth is too narrow for you to cut the belt on the length, it may be cut on the width; but a belt so cut, especially in soft cloths, is prone to stretch and must be stayed inside with a piece of wigan.

Threadmark the hem line at the bottom, and the center line of the dart at the back; also along the front seam if there is to be a kick-pleat at the front. Do not cut the dart; it is to be folded inward on the threadmarks, sewn to the required depth, and pressed sidewise lapping toward the center back.

In cutting skirts, you may use pinking shears along the sides of the panels, but it is better practice to cut everywhere with ordinary shears, overcasting the raw edges afterward.

Basting-up for the try-on

To baste up the skirt for trying-on, proceed as follows:

First, sew the darts in the backparts, on the machine.

Baste together the foreparts of the skirt, having them flat on the bench as you do so. Then baste the backparts together. Next, join the backs to the foreparts at the side seams. Baste neatly and with close stitches, after which turn the skirt inside out and open all the seams with the iron. Finally, rip the left side seam 6 in. down from the top, so that the skirt can be slipped on the body of the wearer.

The baste-up is recommended for the beginner principally to assure getting the seams to lie fair to each other. The use of the sewing machine is risky on these long seams, for it fulls-in the lower layer of cloth onto the upper one, so that the ends are not coincident, and the appearance of the finished seam is a long curve rather than a straight line. But a person experienced in the use of the sewing machine need not do all this basting by hand, and can join the parts together on the machine, using a widened stitch. Such wide-stitched seams are easily ripped open, and have the advantage of forming a straighter, neater, temporary seam than hand basting, and in much shorter time.

The belt is now to be basted on. But first, it must be folded and reinforced inside with a length of wigan. Fold the belt lengthwise, and press it thus flat with the iron. Cut the strip of wigan about 2 in. wide and machine-sew it along the inside edge of the fold of the belt, so that the seaming will not show on the outside of the finished belt.

Baste the skirt onto the belt, not the belt onto the skirt; for there is 1 in. of fullness in the skirt waist (provided by the formula) which must be fulled carefully onto the belt. This fullness is needed because, though the belt must be snug around the waist of the wearer, the body of the skirt below must be sufficiently loose to accommodate the flaring of the hips. In other words, the skirt must be a little larger around the body than the belt is. Yet the fullness must be so distributed that there is no pinching under the seam of the belt. See Fig. 202.

Baste the skirt first onto the edge of the outside fold of the belt. Then turn the belt up in proper position, and baste the inside fold over and inside. The belt should be basted so that 2 in. of it extends beyond each corner of the placket on the left side.

It will be found that basting on the belt properly in relation to the skirt is not always easy. Now and then, the skirt will be a bit too full, and it will be necessary to take it in a trifle at the seams. But it is important to do the job painstakingly, as the drape of the skirt depends mainly on its relation to the belt from which it hangs.

Having finished with the belt, turn up and baste the bottom

in the marks there; then press it, as it is only when the hem is pressed flat that one can judge if the width of the skirt is suitable. Indeed, it is desirable to press the entire skirt before trying it on, as a wrinkled skirt with unpressed seams is impossible to fit accurately. Remember that though a try-on is only a preliminary matter, it is not to be botched and should present a true picture of the finished garment.

At this stage do not concern yourself with the side fastening. When your subject tries on the skirt, you will fasten the side opening with two pins in the position it is planned to close.

Fitting procedure

A skirt is fitted, first, for *size* or *width,* around the waist, around the seat and around the bottom. Assuming that it is on the large side, as it should be for best results, pin out the surplus from the side seams. Pin out equal quantities from each side of the seams, so that you can reduce the skirt by sewing the seams on the double.

The skirt is next fitted for hang or *drape.* This is done by pinning out a horizontal fold around the waist, immediately below the belt, wherever and to whatever extent such pinning out will improve the hang or drape. This pinning out will sometimes be necessary only at the front, sometimes only at the back, and sometimes clear around the waist. It will seldom involve more than ¾ in. of material at the widest; and whatever must be lifted out of the way will pass up under the belt.

Finally, the skirt length is determined by marking all around the bottom the distance it is wanted from the floor. Use a yardstick for this purpose; or better, a regular hem marker.

After the fitting, have your client remove her skirt without taking out any of the pins, which are as yet your only guide in making the alterations. Lay the skirt flat on the table and measure the quantities pinned out, after which remove the pins, and chalk-mark the new run of the seams. Finally, run thread-marks through the chalk marks, to transfer the latter onto the wrong side of the cloth.

Put plenty of time in fitting a skirt. Simple a garment as it is, it requires some pains to plan correctly. Remember, especially if you are a men's tailor, that women are far more particular about the fit of their skirts than men are about the fit of their trousers. Women insist on a fit that is neither tight nor loose over the hips, and ½ in. of excess or deficiency either way is all it takes to relegate the garment to the closet.

Common problems in the fitting of skirts are illustrated in Figs. 190 to 198.

Common problems in fitting skirts

Fig. 190. Normal pattern on wide-hipped figure. Note folds across the front of skirt, indicating a too-long front length in relation to the short side length.

Fig. 191. To remedy the defect, pin a fold out along the front just below the belt, drawing up the excess material. The fold will, of course, be widest at center front, tapering to nothing at the sides.

Fig. 192. Measure the pinned-out fold, and draw a chalk line from hip to hip as shown. The belt will then be seamed on this chalk line.

PROBLEM 1 :- Wide hips

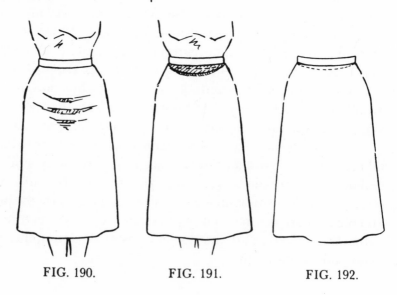

FIG. 190.   FIG. 191.   FIG. 192.

When the seat is flat, it may sometimes be necessary to do this alteration along the back.

PROBLEM 2:– Hips backward

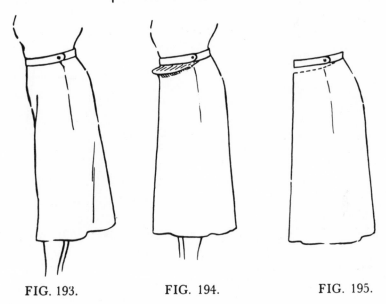

FIG. 193. FIG. 194. FIG. 195.

Fig. 193. Depicts a common trouble with women who carry their hips backward. The normal skirt is too long in front in relation to the back, resulting in the skirt's tipping, as shown.

Fig. 194. To remedy, pin out the fold of excess length along the front, just below the belt and extending a bit beyond the side seams. The extent of excess as indicated by this fold will pass up underneath the belt.

Fig. 195. The chalk line is drawn much as in Fig. 192, and the alteration is worked in the same way.

Fig. 196. Illustrates a common problem with subjects who carry their hips forward. The skirt tips frontward, cupping the buttocks and clinging to the thighs.

Fig. 197. The defect is really the same as Problem 2, and is corrected in the same way.

PROBLEM 3:-Hips forward

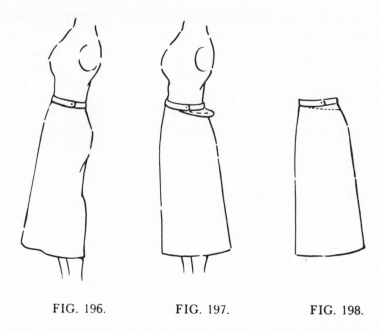

FIG. 196.   FIG. 197.   FIG. 198.

Fig. 198. The excess is marked off along the back, and the belt lowered to the new line.

Assembling, making the pleat, and reducing the skirt

If the skirt has proven correct for size, sew the four panels together on the machine, with a fairly close stitch. Sew in line with the bastings, or a bit outside of them, after which they may be plucked out with the bodkin. On the left side, leave the seam open about 7 in. down where the placket will be; and, if there is to be a kick-pleat at the front, sew down only to the point where it is to open, stopping the thread securely there. Do not yet remove the bastings that close the kick-pleat; this will be done only when the pleat is finished.

The pleat is constructed thus: Cut, on the length of the cloth, a strip 3½ in. wide and about 4 in. longer than the pleat is to open. Turn the skirt inside out, baste this strip congruent onto the pleat inlays (which should be 1½ in. wide), and sew the strip's edges to the inlay edges along both sides. Then turn the skirt right side out and stitch through the top of the pleat in the shape of a peak whose point is a right angle: ⋀ . The thread ends of this peak are drawn through to the reverse side of the skirt and tied securely. See Fig. 201, page 181.

When the skirt has to be reduced in the side seams, measure the quantities pinned out along the seams; then remove the pins, turn the skirt inside out, baste the seams closed, and chalk-mark the new run of seams so that the quantity to be reduced is divided each side of them. By thus reducing as much from the backparts as from the foreparts, the original seam placement and lateral balance of the skirt is retained.

Taking in the skirt in the side seams will, of course, necessitate shortening the belt each side. This can be done in two ways. The most convenient way is to cut the belt at the right side and take a seam there, which when pressed open neatly will not be in the least objectionable. Or — the harder way — the belt can be unbasted clear around the back, and rebasted with the excess length passing beyond the placket, where it may be cut off.

Often, the beginner will be tempted to reduce the skirt at the center-front or center-back seams. This is perfectly proper; but, again, the belt will have to be ripped off almost all around and rebasted so that the excess is diverted toward the placket side. The student will soon learn to avoid all unnecessary ripping of the belt, once it is properly basted, though, of course, he will have to break short sections of the bastings to sew the seams and put in the slide fastener.

Making the placket

Although the placket may be made to close with buttons or snaps, it is most satisfactory when finished with a slide fastener or zipper.

The simplest way, and as good a one as any, to construct a placket is as follows:

Resew the side seam (where the placket will be) with a

widened machine stitch, neatly press open the seam, and baste the closed zipper back of it, along each side. Beginning at the top of the forepart, sew a close-stitched machine seam all around the placket, running it 1/4 in. away from the side seam. Avoid running too close to the teeth of the zipper, as a too-close seam will impede its operation. Make a bar-tack at the base of the zipper, press, and rip open the side seam the length of the placket. You will have a very neatly constructed placket, whose edges when closed will meet evenly and conceal the zipper completely. See Figs. 199 and 200.

You may, if you wish, give an additional finished look to the placket by constructing a small facing and sewing it directly behind the zipper on the backpart side.

Finishing the belt

Once the zipper has been put in, turn your attention to finishing the belt. If it needs to be lowered on the skirt (as in those sections where a horizontal fold of excess has been pinned out) rip and rebaste it in the correct position. Cut the front or buttonhole end of the belt in a peaked shape, providing for a 1/4 in. seam. Fold this end inside out, seam, trim, and turn it outward. The button end of the belt is merely turned in square and may extend an inch beyond the zipper. Finally, neatly turn-in the bottom edge of the inside fold of the belt all around the waist, and seam the belt through the entire length, going through all five thicknesses of cloth.

Making the hem

Turning now to the skirt bottom, rechalk the hemline all around and draw a second line 2 in. below it on which to cut. Cut cleanly, after which sew a length of thin "bias binding" all around the edge. Turn the hem up, basting it loosely in position; then hand-sew all around with loose, close stitches that do not quite penetrate the cloth.

Cut and make a buttonhole in the front end of the belt, and sew a button in proper position on the other end.

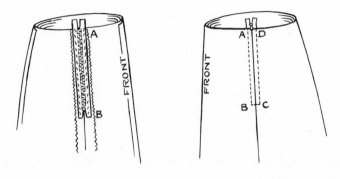

Fig. 199.   Fig. 200.

FIG. 199. The easiest way to make a neat placket. Sew the side seam clear to the top, at A, and press the seam open. Baste the zipper face down on the side seam, as from B to A, each side. FIG. 200. Skirt turned right side out. Stitch from A to B, to C, to D, running the seams ¼ in. each side of the side seam. With a knife, carefully rip open the side seam the length of the zipper, A-B. (A small facing may be stitched back of the zipper, along B-C-D.)

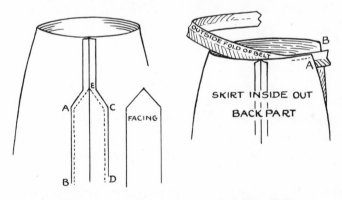

Fig. 201.   Fig. 202.

FIG. 201. A simple method of making a pleat. Cut the skirt with an additional 1¾ in. of material each side of the forepart at the front. Stitch the center-front seam clear to the bottom. Cut a facing to the shape of A-B-C-D-E and baste it congruent onto it. Stitch the two layers each side, as from B to A and C to D. Stitch the peak, C-E-A, through all layers. FIG. 202. How to baste and stitch on the belt. Turn the skirt inside out. Start basting at the back corner of the placket, at A, holding the belt face to face with the skirt. Lay the skirt on the sewing machine, belt uppermost, and stitch from A clear around to B.

181

Chapter XI

Women's Coat Making

Although women's figures are commonly assumed to be very different in overall proportions from men's, comparative measurements will demonstrate that, except for her rounded breasts and wider pelvis, a woman's physique much resembles that of a young male's.

A man's 34-chest coat pattern, for example, can easily be converted into a woman's 34-chest 36-bust pattern by the simple expedients of splitting the shoulder and introducing into the breast region a triangle of added material for bust provision. This triangle is a designing feature common to all garments for women.

The difference between the chest and bust measurements, and the methods of taking both, are shown in Fig. 16, Page 43. For the average woman it can be assumed without measuring at all that her bust will be about 2 in. larger than her chest.

Also, a woman's fitted coat generally has much more waist suppression than a man's which makes it much more shapely. And generally a short dart is stitched down the center of the back shoulders to "round" them out a bit in keeping with the characteristic roundness of the female back shoulder.

182

It should be noticed that in most cutting systems for women's coats, seams are not all included in the pattern as they are in men's patterns, but in the formula here presented, *seams of ⅜ in. are provided throughout.* Note, also, that the woman's coat is drafted by the *bust scale* rather than by the chest scale.

Directions for taking measurements for a woman's jacket are included in the instructions on page 43, but for best results the present draft should be reproduced in the 36-bust size and to the other dimensions given here. The proportionate pattern thus obtained can then be graded into bust sizes 34, 38, and 40, much in the same way as was the man's coat pattern in Chapter VII, Fig. 22(a-d).

The fitting of a woman's coat follows the same procedure as fitting the man's. Therefore study well the material on pages 67-76 relative to fitting at the try-on stage.

WOMAN'S COAT FORMULA

Chest, 34 in.   Half-back, 7¼ in.
Bust, 36 in.   Waist, 26 in.
Back length, 24 in.   Hips, 40 in.
Armhole depth, 8½ in.   Height, 5'4"-5'6"

Bust scale, 18 in.
All quantities proportionate; ⅜ in. seams provided
throughout.

Draw perpendicular line 1-2 the length of the coat (24 in.).

3 from 1 is the armhole depth (8½ in. for this size).

4 from 1 is the waist depth (15½ in.).

Square out from 1, 2, 3, and 4.

5 from 1 is half the bust measure plus 7 in. (18 plus 7, or 25 in.).

8 is the same. Rule line 5-8.

9 is midway between 3 and 6. Square down from 9.

10 from 9 is ¼ bust scale (4½ in.). Square up and down.

11 from 9 is half of 9-10 (2¼ in.). Square up.

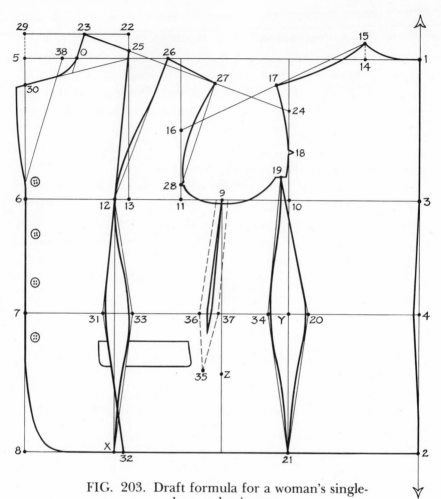

FIG. 203. Draft formula for a woman's single-
breasted suit coat.

12 from 11 is ¼ bust scale (4½ in.). Square down.

13 from 12 is ¼ of 11-12 (1¼ in.). Square up and beyond top line toward 22.

This is the basic scaffolding and should be checked very carefully for utmost accuracy.

14 from 1 is ⅙ scale plus ⅜ in. (3⅜ in.). Square up.

15 above 14 is ⅞ in. Curve from 15 into 1 as suggested.

16 is midway between 11 and the top line. Rule 15 to 16.

17 is ½ in. from the vertical line. Curve gently from 17 to 5, running the curve ⅜ in. below line 15-17.

18 is ⅙ scale above 10 and is the location of the back notch for the sleeve. Cut a nick in the pattern here.

19 is 1¼ in. above 10 and ⅜ in. from the vertical line. Draw horizontally through point 19, as shown.

20 is 1 in. from the vertical line. Rule 19 to 20 and 20 to 21.

Curve into 20 very gently and a bit outside hip line, 20-21.

Rule from 3 to a point ¼ in. inside 4 and down toward 2, as suggested, for a bit of waist suppression there. This completes the backpart.

22 is normally 1⅝ in. above the top line of the draft. Square from 22 toward 29.

23 from 22 is half the distance from 15 to 17 (3 in.).

24 above 10 is ⅓ scale (6 in.). Rule 23 to 24.

Rule from 25, through 12, and to 31.

26 is ¾ in. from the vertical line near it. Rule 26 to 12 and 26 to 27.

27 from 26 is half the distance from 15 to 17 plus ½ in. (3½ in.).

28 above 11 is 1 in. and this point is the notch for the sleeve inseam.

Rule 27 to 28 and curve the armhole ½ in. inside this line as suggested in the draft. Continue the curve from 28 to 29 and up to a point ⅜ in. from 19, as shown.

30 below 29 is ⅙ scale (3 in.). Rule 30 to top line just below 25.

Square down obliquely from 23 by resting the elbow of the square on point 23 with its arm resting on line 23-25. Curve from 23 to 30 as suggested.

31 is 1¼ in. from the vertical line there.

32 is ½ in. from point X. Rule 31 to 32.

33 is 1¼ in. from vertical. Rule 12-33 and 33-X. Curve the line outwardly above and below point 12, no more than

¼ in. at the most. Curve inwardly at 33 and outwardly again toward point 32.

34 from Y is 1⅜ in. Rule 19 to 34 and 34 to 21. Faintly curve the line from 19 to 34, and also over the hip from 34 to 21.

35 is about 4 in. below 36 and 1½ in. from the vertical line at Z. Draw line 9 to 35.

36 is about 1¼ in. from the vertical line at 37. Rule from points which are ⅜ in. on both sides of 9, into 36 and 37. Then rule from 36 to 35 and 37 to 35. In cutting, you may cut from 9 to about 1½ in. below the waistline. The thing to remember is that a total of ¾ in. is to be sewn out at 9 and a total of 1½ in. to be sewn out between 36 and 37, attenuating the seam into a point at 35.

38 is ¾ in. from O. Rule from 38 to a point about 1½ in above 6. This locates the crease of revers.

The revers juts out an additional ¼ in. at 30 and is slightly curved, not a straight line.

The coat front at 8 may be rounded as shown, unless it is preferred square.

The topmost button is to be 1½ in. above 6, and the bottom button 2 in. below 7, the four buttons being 3¼ in. apart.

The top of the flap or mouth of the pocket is to be 2¼ in. below the waistline.

Designing the back shoulder with a dart

A woman's jacket can often be satisfactorily made with the back of the shoulder undarted as in the draft, Fig. 203. However, since most women are a bit rounded over the back shoulder, many tailors prefer to introduce the back shoulder dart in the pattern. One method of doing this is shown in Fig. 204.

Take the backpart of the pattern you have produced from Fig. 203 and reproduce on it the numerals of the draft, 15, 17, and 18.

A from 15 is 2½ in.

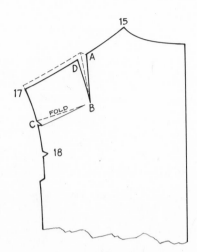

FIG. 204. Designing the back
shoulder with a dart.

B below A is 3¼ in. and B from scye line 17-18 is 3¼ in.
Draw line A-B and cut down through it.

C is 2½ in. down from 17. Fold out at C a total of ½ in.
from the pattern, folding in the form of a wedge with its
point at B. Staple this fold closed, which will cause the
pattern to open ½ in. at A-D, and introduce the dart which
you will later sew out.

A ½-in. strip of pattern should be added along and above
points 17 to D to raise the shoulder a bit there. Or you could
make this slight addition when marking the backpart on the
cloth.

The dart is not cut through. Simply threadmark it down
the center and stitch it in a fold, making the point sharp.

THE COLLAR DRAFT

The size here given is for the 36-bust jacket with revers.
It can be enlarged by adding a bit more length at 5-7 and a
bit more width at 1-7. The addition is ⅛ in. for every
increase in bust size.

1 from 2 is 3 in.

Square out from 1 to 3 and from 2 to 4.

3 from 1 is 8 in.

4 from 2 is 5¼ in.

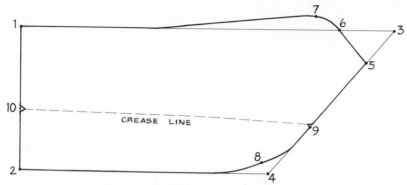

FIG. 205. The Collar Formula.

Rule from 3 to 4.

5 from 4 is 3 in.

6 from 1 is 6¾ in.

7 is ¼ in. above the line. Curve as suggested toward 1 and into 6.

8 is ¼ in. from 4. Curve through 8 up to 9, as shown.

9 is 1¾ in. from 5; 10 is 1¾ in. from 1.

Notch at 9 and 10 which locates the crease of the collar and where it joins the crease of the revers.

THE SLEEVE FORMULA

To be drafted by the chest scale of the coat.

Scale, 18 in.

Sleeve inseam, 17 in.

Sleeve bottom, 10 in. around.

The topside

Rule the perpendicular line, 1 to 2, about 24 in. long.

Square out from 1 to Y.

3 below 1 is ⅓ scale (6 in. in this draft).

4 below 3 is the inseam measure (17 in.). Square out from 4.

5 is midway between 3 and 4. Square out to 9, the elbow.

6 above 3 is ⅙ scale (3 in. in this draft).

7 is ¾ in. above 3 and locates the sleeve notch.

8 from 7, measured on the slant, is ½ the scale (8¾ in.).

188

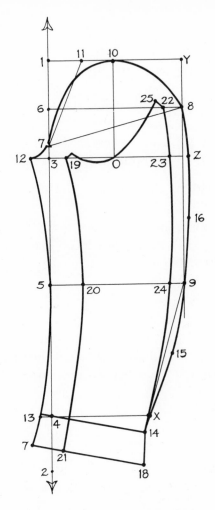

FIG. 206. The Sleeve Formula.

Rule 7 to 8.

8 from 6 in this draft is 8⅝ in., and 9 from 5 is the same.
Rule 9 to 8 and up to Y.

10 is midway between 1 and Y.

0 is midway between 3 and Z. Rule from 10 to 0.

11 is midway between 1 and 10. Rule from 11 to 7, and
curve the topsleeve as suggested, from 8 into 10, to 7.

12 is 1 in. from 3, and 13 is 1 in. from 4.

Draw curved line 12-5-13.

14 from 11 is 7 in.; 14 below X is 1¼ in.

Rule 13 to 14 and 14 to 9.

Draw a gently curved line down from 8, into 9, and down to 14.

The curve should run outside the line about ¼ in. at points 15 and 16.

17 and 18 are 2 in. below 13 and 14, and this addition is for the turn-in of the bottom. Rule from 17 to 18.

The underside

19 from 3 is 1¼ in.

20 from 5 is 2 in.

21 from 13 is 2 in. Draw curved line 19-20-21.

22 from 8 is 1½ in.

23 from Z is 1¼ in.

24 from 9 is ¾ in.

Draw the curved line, 22-23-24-14.

25 is ¼ in. above the line and ½ in. from 22.

Rule 25 to 0, and curve ¼ in. below the line between 19 and 0. Continue the curve to a point ¼ in. above the line at 19.

Cut out the topside; then superimpose it on another sheet of paper, and with a tracing wheel or a sharp nail, mark through and around the underside, 19-20-21-18-24-23-22-25-0-19. Then cut out the undersleeve. For additional information on sleeves, see the material on men's sleeves.

Grading the pattern

In the chapter on men's coat making, you read about how patterns are "graded," enlarged or reduced progressively in a range of sizes. The woman's coat is treated in the same way, except that the front part is graded ⅛ in. for each size down its front (as well as at the top and bottom), and the side-front is graded ⅛ in. for each size along its front side, 26-12-33-X, and along its back side, 19-34-21. All other parts are graded exactly as is the man's coat.

Once grading is understood, a well-proportioned, 36-bust pattern can be used to cut coats in a range of sizes from 34 to 42 bust. The author proved this in working with a class of twenty-four women differing in sizes, by giving them an identical 36-bust pattern which they were taught to enlarge or reduce, each to her own size. All made excellent coats for themselves.

Making the front canvases

The pattern for your canvas interlinings is composed of three parts (Fig. 207): *Part A,* which is the replica of the coat front or forepart; *Part B,* which is the replica of the coat side-front, with its lower portions cut off from the bottom of the armhole down to the level of the pocket at X; and *Part C,* a piece the width of the shoulder, slanted at the top, with a cut-out wedge at center bottom for breast shape.

Parts A and B should be cut about ½ in. wider and longer than the patterns. They may be made out of medium or heavy weight hymo canvas, obtainable at most fabric stores. The hymo is laid folded lengthwise on the bench and the parts are cut on the length (not on the bias).

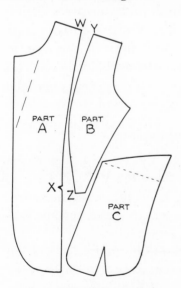

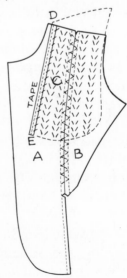

FIG. 207. Pattern for canvas underlinings.

FIG. 208. Making the front canvases.

191

To construct the canvases (Fig. 208), first cut two inch-wide strips of silesia a bit longer than W to X of Part A. Machine-stitch Part A from W to X onto one of these strips. Then machine-stitch Part B from Z to Y onto the strip, edge to edge with Part A, X-W. Then stitch zigzag-fashion down the entire seam to seal the two edges against each other smoothly.

The canvas will now need additional firmness over the round of the breasts and across the shoulders. This is to be provided by Part C.

First, machine-stitch the little bottom dart of Part C onto a strip of silesia, closing it edge to edge and then stitching zigzag-fashion down its whole length. Next, baste Part C to the top area of the canvas so that its slanted top protrudes above the shoulder level, and its front edge, D-E, lies about ½ in. inside the crease of the revers. (It must never extend into the front or gorge of the coat so that it prevents the revers from turning.)

Work Part C all over with loose padding stitches in up-and-down rows, the first of which should be run down the center. Moisten with a damp sponge and dry-press, being careful to retain the breast roundness. Machine-stitch a stay-tape from E to D, stitching down both sides of the tape to cover the canvas edge and keep it unstretchable there. You may then machine-stitch strips of thin material over the other edges of Part C, but not along the top of the shoulder. Part C always faces the inside lining of the coat, as does the shoulder pad which is hand-basted at the top.

Note that the length of the edge Y-Z of Part B must be exactly the same as the length of the edge W-X of Part A. You should measure both edges with the tape measure, following the curved contours of each to make certain that they are the same length.

While on the subject of canvases, it might be well to explain why I have advocated a bias-cut canvas in the chapter on men's coat making, while here I advocate one cut on the warp or "straight" of the hymo. This is really an optional matter over which there need be no controversy. The older school of tailors cut their canvases on the bias because they believed that there was less danger from shrinkage that way and because the front edges of the coat could be drawn in and pressed better with the heavy canvas materials that they then used. In recent years, however, when lighter hymos have been put into coats, straight-cut canvases which are well preshrunk have been found to function as well, if not better, than the bias-cut ones. In the present edition of this book, I have seen no reason to change the instructions in Chapter VII. It is one method of making good canvases, but there is nothing wrong with cutting canvases on the straight, and, in fact, the pre-cut commercial canvases supplied by tailors' trimming houses for both men's and women's coats are generally cut on the straight.

The use of haircloth, too, has largely been abandoned in recent years because the thinner suitings used do not require it. But an extra layer of hymo in the breast area is required to replace it in both men's and women's suit coats. In men's overcoats, however, haircloth can still be used to advantage.

Pocket and buttonhole making (bound or jetted style)

The making of flapped pockets and hand-stitched button-holes has already been covered in the chapter on men's coat making. However, since both pockets and buttonholes may also be constructed in "bound" fashion on women's coats, instructions for making them are given here. Start practicing pocket making on oddments of cloth rather than on a coat you are making. It is easy to spoil a coat front with poorly made pockets or buttonholes.

Fig. 209. First chalk-line the mouth of your pocket, X-X, about 5¼ in. long, so that it barely passes through the front seam, A. It may, but need not, extend across side seam, B, as in the figure. The pocket mouth must be aligned parallel with the coat bottom and about 8½ in. above it.

Having drawn this line, turn to the insides of fronts and baste an oblong piece of thin unstretchable cloth, such as wigan or lining material, 7 x 3 in. in size, opposite the line X-X. This is to act as a stay to prevent the finished pocket mouth from stretching—and is most important.

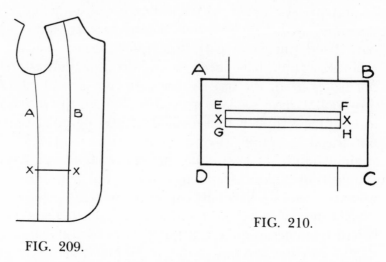

FIG. 209.

FIG. 210.

Fig. 210. Now cut an oblong piece of cloth on the length or warp of the material 7 x 3 in. in size. Baste it over X-X; then transfer the line X-X onto it. Chalk a second line, E-F, ¼ in. above X-X; then chalk a third line, G-H, ¼ in. below X-X. Chalk a vertical line squarely at each pocket end, F-H and E-G. You may then machine-stitch around the oblong E-F-G-H, going through all layers. (Remember that the cloth piece, A-B-C-D, is of the same material as the coat and is placed on it face side down.)

Fig. 211. Start cutting through all layers at the center of line X-X. Cut toward each end, snipping into each corner of the oblong, as shown, but being very careful not to cut through the stitchings there.

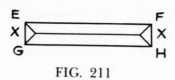

FIG. 211

194

Fig. 212. This shows the reverse or inside of the coat. You have inserted your finger inside the pocket mouth and drawn in the oblong piece, A-B-C-D, inside the coat. You may then press open the seams E-F and G-H, as shown.

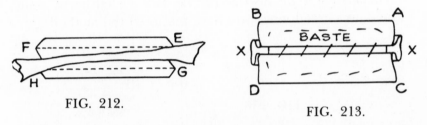

FIG. 212.

FIG. 213.

Fig. 213. Baste the oblong, A-B-C-D, first from the outside of the coat from E to F and G to H. Then from the inside of the coat, close the mouth of the pocket temporarily with a loose basting. Next, press again from inside the coat, pulling out the ends at X-X (to draw the little points of the pocket ends outwardly).

Fig. 214. This shows how the coat front is turned over to machine-stitch across the little points and make strong, neat pocket ends. Note that the pocket silesia has been attached at J.

Fig. 215. Next, machine-stitch onto the outside pocket directly in the ridge of the seam G-H. This is a finished seam, and you should leave the threads long at each end, then draw them through to the reverse of the coat and tie them well.

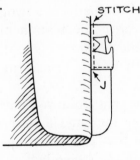

FIG. 214.

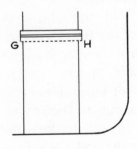

FIG. 215.

Fig. 216. The finished pocket is shown here from the reverse of the coat. The facing piece, also 7 x 3 in., has been stitched to the silesia, then basted to the pocket, and the finish seam taken from outside the coat as from H to F, across to E, and down to G.

Pockets made in this way can be constructed horizontally, slanted, or curved, once you have mastered the method.

FIG. 216.

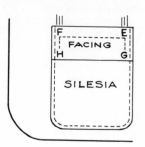

Buttonholes

Buttonholes of the bound type are made in the very same way as shown in Figs. 209-216. They should be chalk-lined very carefully, drawing the three lines little more than ⅛ in. apart so as to make the buttonhole no more than ⅜ in. wide vertically. Horizontally, they should be marked ⅛ in. wider than the buttons you will use.

Such buttonholes must always be made *before* the coat facing is attached. They are machine-stitched right through the canvas, which then "stays" them. It stands to reason, therefore, that a too-heavy or stiff canvas material should not be used in a coat in which such holes are to be made.

Buttonholes are often four in number on a woman's coat. The top button is on a line with the bottom of the revers; the bottom one is level with the pocket mouth. Middle buttons are spaced evenly between these two, usually about 3 or 2¾ in. apart.

After buttonholes are made in the coat front, you may add the facings to the fronts, constructing the latter as shown on pages 89-92. In fact, only after the coat is finished and the fronts pressed is it safe to cut through the facing behind each buttonhole, much as in Fig. 211, center line. You may very slightly nick the ends in little points as shown in Fig. 211. Then turn in the facing on the line E-F-G-H, hand-stitching finely around each buttonhole from the facing side, finishing the back of the buttonhole in the shape of a tiny oblong.

Completing the woman's coat: A word to women students

Other than the foregoing instructions on the cutting of women's coats, the making of canvases for them, and the construction of jetted pockets and buttonholes, the making of the coat proceeds exactly as the making of a man's coat. Therefore, the student should study well the chapter on men's coat making as a preparation for women's garment making. Indeed, since the male form is the easier to clothe and fit, the serious woman student will do well to make her first coat for some male relative.

Your male subject will be perfectly content with a loose, straight-hanging garment, but he will be exacting about its cut and construction. In any case, his criticism will be good discipline for you, and once you have satisfied him, you will be better prepared to put into your women's coats the desirable features found in men's clothing.

I take exception to the statement that a woman's coat is radically different from a man's. True, it has more curvature to provide for the larger breasts and hips, but otherwise the woman's coat is constructed basically like the man's.

Style variations

The coat pattern produced from the formula in this chapter possesses the conservative fitted character on which many style variations can be imposed. One can make it longer or shorter, vary the pockets, add cuffs to the sleeves, alter the shape of the revers, etc. One might even make from it a button-to-throat coat with a rounded "Peter Pan" collar. But, as far as learning coat making is concerned, it is far best for the student to make her first coats with revers, as here, and with the type of collar given in Fig. 205.

Supplementary Material

PUTTING ON THE OUTSIDE COLLAR BY HAND

O<small>N</small> PAGES 110-113, a rapid method of sewing on the outside collar by machine was shown. This is the easier method for beginners, but it does not attain the high standard of tailoring that the hand-felled collar does. I, therefore, present the main steps in sewing on the collar by hand.

Fig. 217. **Trim the undercollar the exact shape and size it is to finish, cutting through both canvas and undercollar** cloths. Then trim the canvas ⅛ in. inside the undercollar cloth edge all around, A-B-C-D. **The canvas is shown trimmed in** this illustration.

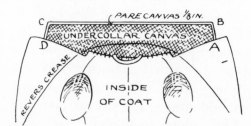

FIG. 217. Paring the canvas.

Fig. 218. Cut the outside collar about 1 in. wider all around than is the undercollar. Baste the outside collar around the edge, A to B, to C, to D. Baste also along the break of the collar, A-F-G-D. Trim edge to an even ½ in. turn-in all around.

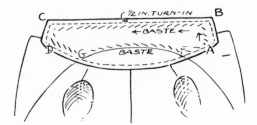

FIG. 218. Basting on the
outside collar.

Fig. 219. Turn and baste edge of the outside collar flush against the top edge of the revers, as at A to F. Continue turning thus from F to G and to D.

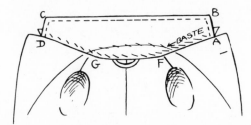

FIG. 219. Turning the
bottom edge.

Fig. 220. Start turning in the edge of the outside collar from the corner, A, basting very evenly and making a small, rounded corner at B. This drawing shows only part of the collar thus turned in; the edge must, of course, be turned clear to C and D. When this is done, hand-fell the collar to the revers, as from A to F, to D, to G. Take very fine, close stitches in this seam, as the stitches should not show after the pressing. Then, turning to the back of the collar, hand-fell the under-collar edge to that of the outside collar, as from D to C, to B, to A. This, too, should be done with fine, close stitches. Finally, tack the undercollar especially firmly at the corners, A and D.

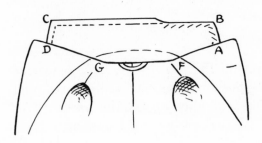

FIG. 220. Turning the
upper edge and ends.

All this basting and hand sewing take a lot of time, but tailors striving after excellence in their garment have been putting this work in their collars for centuries. The object is to obtain the thinnest collar edge possible. To get an idea of good collar construction, examine the collars on coats constructed by the better makers.

HOW TO MAKE PATCH POCKETS—FIGS. 221-224

Fig. 221. The pocket is here shown wrong side up. The dashed lines represent the outline of the finished pocket. A length of staytape is first machine-sewn across the top, just above the fold line, A-B. A piece of silesia cut a bit wider than the pocket each side, but 1 in. shorter lengthwise, is sewn as from C to D.

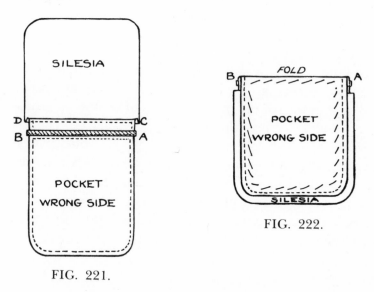

FIG. 221.

FIG. 222.

Fig. 222. Fold pocket on the top line, A-B, face to face with the silesia. Baste the pocket to the silesia all around, and then trim the silesia even with the edge of the pocket. This illustration shows the silesia basted but not trimmed.

Fig. 223. The pocket is here shown turned over with the silesia trimmed all around. Lay the pocket on the sewing machine, silesia uppermost, and stitch a narrow seam from B to C to D, leaving the area from D to E unstitched, and continuing the seam from E to A. Push the bodkin through the opening between D and E, and turn the pocket right side out. Baste around the edges, turning the silesia a bit inside the cloth edge. Close the opening, D-E, sewing it by hand.

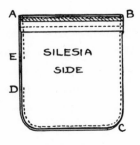

FIG. 223.

Fig. 224. **Press the pocket, and stitch a ¼ in. finish seam across the top from A to B. A and B are each ¼ in. from the edge, and the thread ends are left long there to be pulled through and tied from the back. Baste the pocket to the coat all around, and stitch a ¼ in. edge seam from B to C, to D, to A. The corners at A and B are reinforced from the** reverse of the coat with invisible tacks.

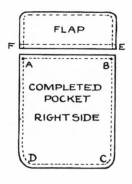

FIG. 224.

It is a good idea to cut templates out of heavy cardboard for repeated use in cutting such patches.

A man's side pocket patch measures 6¾ in. across the top, and 8 in. vertically. His breast pocket patch measures 4¾ in. by 5½ in. Flaps for the side pockets measure 7 in. by 2¼ in. None of these dimensions includes seams, and they hold only for a coat of average size. The larger the coat, the larger the pockets.

Flaps are stitched as from E to F, which is a line ¾ in. above the top edge of the pocket. They are then turned down and stitched a ¼ in. finish seam across the top, thus covering the raw edge.

MISCELLANEOUS NOTES

For the first try-on of a coat, most tailors have the collar basted on if only to give an indication as to how it will influence the hang of the garment. This is wise practice even if the collar has to be ripped off immediately and reset. For a coat tried without a collar has a tendency to slide frontward on the shoulders, giving the impression that the foreparts are too long in relation to the back.

There is no more certain a way of setting the collar right than to pin it onto the coat at the first try-on. Immediately after you have pinned the coat fronts closed, pin the collar at the center-back seam. Pin it over the left shoulder to the revers crease, then across the right shoulder. Turn down the collar and pin its ends to the revers at the desired angle, as shown in Fig. 104. In doing this work, the original outlines of the collar are ignored, and any surplus length or width at the ends is pared away later. The only care is to have the crease of the collar running continuously into the crease of the revers.

It is not safe to assume that a size 40 sleeve will be correct for the armhole of a man's size 40 coat, due to variations in armhole depth and width. The careful tailor measures around the stayed armhole of the coat and produces a sleeve with a hole measuring 2¾ in. (2 in. for a woman's coat) more than that quantity.

The young tailor will find it profitable to invest in proved proportionate patterns in chest size 40 for a male figure and in bust size 36 for a female. These are the median sizes from which one can cut garments for smaller or larger figures. Get these patterns in the conservative style from a reputable designer. Get some inexpensive cloth and cut coats on each pattern. Sew them up roughly with canvases basted in the fronts, and with collars, but without sleeves and facings. By trying one of these model coats on your subject, you will obtain a very good idea of the changes that you should make in the base pattern for his or her figure.

The young craftsman should also know what a proportionate man or woman measures, and should work on the proportionate figure before attempting to deal with abnormalities. As regards male subjects, it is useful to bear the following data in mind:

Measurements taken on a large number of males in the military service show the most common chest measure to lie between 39 and 40. Waists, on the average, measure 5 in. less than chests, and seats 1 or 2 in. larger than chests. The tailor therefore conceives the proportionate male figure as about 40 in. around the chest, 35 in. around the waist, and about 42 in. around the seat. Coats designated as "regulars" in the ready-made trade are designed close to these proportions.

Of course, many young men have waists 6 in. or more smaller than their chests, and seats the equal of or smaller than their chests, but it is best to have a too-loose coat in the waist and seat regions than one too small. We can always easily reduce garments in these sections.

The average woman's proportions may be summed as follows: Her chest measures between 35 and 36 in. Her breast (or bust) is 2 in. or more larger than her chest. Her waist is 5 in. or more smaller than her chest. Her seat is 6 in. or more larger than her chest. We may therefore conceive of the average female figure as 36 chest, 38 breast, 31 waist, and 42 seat. There are, of course, many women with smaller waists and seats than this in proportion to their chests, but again it is best to favor the larger measurement.

If you must have your finished suits pressed on a pressing machine, make certain that the operator is experienced in pressing new garments. A competent operator will be careful to retain the chest shape in the coat — a most important matter, especially in women's coats. He will first press the garment dry, even to the shiny stage. When it has set for some time, he will steam it a bit to remove the gloss. The sleeve he will press lying against the body of the coat, in its natural position. The collar he will press on the end of the board. Good machine pressing is preferable to poor flatiron pressing, but it is well to do your best at hand pressing before relinquishing garments to the machine. There are areas in coats which the average machine pressman cannot reach or treat adequately.

Finely done hand-sewing has always been regarded as the hallmark of superior tailoring, but from the standpoint of durability it is not preferable to machine-stitching. If you examine your old garments, you will discover that it is the **hand-stitching that has fallen** apart first. For this reason, do **hand-sewing only** where you must. For example, avoid sewing **elaborate "double curtains"** in your trousers tops. Under hard **wear,** such appendages soon unfasten and become just so much loose material to get tangled in. Sew a simple waistband lining as advocated in this book, and the garments will wear the better.

The best tailoring practice is the simplest. Do not be impressed by elaborate methods of working which defy analysis. You should always know why you are doing something in the way you do it. The apprentices of a century ago could be excused for following the instructions of their masters blindly, but the modern literate student does not need to go through rituals that he does not understand.

To stretch a collar (or any other edge), moisten area with the sponge, set the moderately hot iron firmly to the right of the area, and do the stretching with the left hand exclusively. The stretching occurs directly in front of the iron as it travels to and fro across the area, drying the cloth as it spreads. A collar cut in the manner taught in this book needs very little stretching. Indeed, many tailors do not stretch it at all until it is completed and the coat is being pressed.

Most tailors line their sleeves before sewing them into the coat. Many also finish the sleeve bottoms completely. For the beginner, it is best to do neither, in case the sleeve needs altering in width or length after being set.

Be careful how you draw out bastings. Thread forcibly drawn out can cut the cloth just as surely as can a sharp knife. Unfasten the ends of the bastings and draw them out gently with the bodkin.

To see if cloth is wool (assuming that you cannot tell wool by its feel) cut off a little piece and set a lighted match to it. Wool doesn't catch fire; it only singes. Do not hold the cloth clipping in your hand while lighting it, for if it is composed of synthetic materials it may burst suddenly into flames and burn your fingers.

Cloth may be shrunk by steaming it on the pressing machine, as well as by wrapping it in damp sheets. Either hot or cold moisture will shrink woolens. (This is well to remember in laundering trousers or sweaters. If you do not want them to shrink, wash them in lukewarm water and do not hang them out in the cold air or under a hot sun. Choose a temperate day.)

Glossary

ALPACA. A thin cloth made of the wool of Alpaca sheep.

BASTING. Fastening cloth with wide stitches, to be removed later, preliminary to actual sewing.

BEATER. A wooden paddle, used to flatten obstinate cloth in pressing.

BIAS. The diagonal of the cloth.

BLIND STITCH. A stitch that does not pass completely through the cloth and is invisible from the right side.

BODKIN. A bone pencil used to pull out bastings.

BREAK (OF REVERS). Seam joining revers to collar end.

BRIDLE. A strip of unstretchable material sewn in the canvas in line with the crease of revers.

CANVAS. Usually refers to the interlining or foundation of coat front.

CHEESEBLOCK. A semicircular block of wood, perfectly smooth and padded in the manner of a press-board. It is used to press sections of the coat as it is being built.

CREASE OF LAPEL. The crease formed by the turning of the revers over the coat front.

DRAWING-IN. Shortening the edge of material by drawing a thread through and along it.

DRILLING. A heavy twilled cotton material, used for making pockets.

FACINGS. Inside portions of garments that are made from the cloth rather than lining.

FALL OF COLLAR. The part of the collar which folds down from the crease edge.

FELLING. Sewing by hand one piece of material onto another.

FULLING-ON. Distributing the excess material of a longer length of cloth onto a shorter one.

GORGE. The front part of the coat adjacent to the throat.

HAIRCLOTH. A stiff material whose woof is made of the hair of the tails and manes of horses.

HAIRVAS. An interlining material now widely marketed in whicn the hair and wool are interwoven for increased resilience.

HEM. Any edge folded in and felled, as the bottom of a coat.

INLAYS. Extra cloth allowed outside seams to permit enlargement of garment.

LAPEL. The entire front edge of the coat; not to be confused with revers.

LAYING-ON FAIR. Sewing equal lengths of material one onto the other so that their ends coincide.

NOTCH OF LAPEL. The top of the revers from its corner to the edge of the collar.

NOTCHES (SAME AS NICKS.) Shallow cuts guiding the tailor in setting sleeves, and sewing trouser legs. Patterns are *notched*, that is, small wedges are cut out with two snips of the shears; cloth is *nicked* with a single snip.

ON THE DOUBLE. Cloth lying in two layers, or folded.

OPENING THE PATTERN. Increasing a section of the pattern by cutting it open and introducing a wedge.

OVERCASTING. Sewing along the raw or sheared edge of cloth to prevent raveling.

PIPECLAY. Tailor's chalk.

PIPED SEAM. A seam whose edges are covered with a narrow strip of thin lining material.

PITCH OF SLEEVE. The angle at which the sleeves fall from the armhole.

PURL. The knot of the buttonhole stitch.

RAW EDGE. The cut or sheared edge of cloth.

REVERS. The part of the coat front that turns over, erroneously termed lapel.

SACK COAT. A term derived from the French *sacque* referring to any coat of loose cut.

SCYE. An ancient word for the armhole.

SELVEDGE. The machined edge of the cloth bolt.

SILESIA. A tough, twilled, cotton cloth used for making pockets in coats.

SKELETON LINING. A quarter lining, or any other style of sparse lining in a coat.

STAND OF COLLAR. The portion of the collar rising from the neck seam and extending to the crease edge.

STAYS. Unstretchable strips of material used to reinforce edges.

STRAIGHT OF CLOTH. The cloth as running up and down; along the warp.

TACK OR BAR-TACK. Heavy thread sewn across the ends of pocket mouths and other openings, for reinforcement.

TRIMMINGS. A term applied to all materials going into a garment, aside from the cloth proper.

TWILL WEAVE. A weave characterized by a close, diagonal pattern.

VENT. An opening in the center back seam of coat, over the seat. Also refers to the opening of the sleeve bottom.

WIGAN. A stiff, cotton material used for staying pockets and to give body to the fronts and sleeve bottoms of coats.

Index